WILDLIFE
and PLANTS
of the world

An updated and expanded edition of *Wildlife of the World*

now including plants, microorganisms, and biomes

Volume 11

Marshall Cavendish
New York • London • Toronto • Sydney

Marshall Cavendish Corporation
99 White Plains Road
Tarrytown, New York 10591-9001

© Marshall Cavendish Corporation, 1999

Created by **Brown Partworks Ltd**

Library of Congress Cataloging-in-Publication Data

Wildlife and plants of the world.
   p.   cm.
   Includes bibliographical references and index.
   Summary: Alphabetically-arranged illustrated articles introduce over 350 animals, plants, and habitats and efforts to protect them.
   ISBN 0-7614-7099-9 (set : lib. bdg. : alk. paper)
   1. Animals—Juvenile literature. 2. Plants—Juvenile literature.
[1. Animals. 2. Plants.] I. Marshall Cavendish Corporation.
   QL49.W539   1998
   578—DC21   97-32139
                                                        CIP
                                                        AC

ISBN 0-7614-7099-9 (set)
ISBN 0-7614-7110-3 (vol.11)

Printed in Malaysia
Bound in the United States

Brown Packaging

Editorial consultants:
   • Joshua Ginsberg, Ph.D.
   • Jefferey Kaufmann, Ph.D.
   • Paul Sieswerda, Ph.D.
     (Wildlife Conservation Society)
   • Special thanks to the Dept. of Botany,
     The Natural History Museum, U.K.

Editors: Deborah Evans
                                   Leon Gray
Assistant editor: Amanda Harman
Art editors: Joan Curtis
                                   Alison Gardner
                                   Sandra Horth
Picture researchers: Amanda Baker
                                   Brenda Clynch
Illustrations: Bill Botten
                                   John Francis

Marshall Cavendish Corporation

Editorial director: Paul Bernabeo
Project editor: Debra M. Jacobs
Editorial consultant: Elizabeth Kaplan

PICTURE CREDITS
The publishers would like to thank Natural History Photographic Agency, Ardingly, Sussex, U.K., for supplying the following pictures:
Agence Nature 698; A.N.T. (Bruce Thomson) 687, 702; Anthony Bannister 657, 660, 661, 674; G. I. Bernard 678, 679, 655; Laurie Campbell 695, 658; James H. Carmichael Jr. 682; Stephen Dalton 676, 677; Manfred Danegger 692, 693, 696, 697; Nigel J. Dennis 656, 669; Douglas Dickins 703; Patrick Fagot 648; Jeff Goodman 698; Daniel Heuclin 650; E. A. Janes 666; Peter Johnson 690; Stephen Krasemann 662, 663, 685; Gerard Lacz 673, 700; David Middleton 647; Haroldo Palo 654, 686; William S. Paton 668; Dr. Ivan Polunin 675; E. Hanumantha Rao 681; Andy Rouse 665; Jany Sauvenet 664, 672; Kevin Schafer 651; John Shaw 646, 659, 667, 684; Morten Strange 649; Karl Switak 671; Roger Tidman 670; David Woodfall 694.

Additional pictures supplied by:
Frank Lane Picture Agency 652, 680, 683, 691, 701; Oxford Scientific Films 699; Planet Earth Pictures 653, 688.

Front cover
Main image: Giant panda eating bamboo, photographed by Jany Sauvenet.
Additional image: Cattleya orchid, photographed by Kevin Schafer.

Status

In the Key Facts on the species described in this publication, you will find details of the appearance, name (both Latin and common name wherever possible), breeding habits, and so on. The status of an organism indicates how common it is. The status of each organism is based on reference works prepared by two organizations: *1996 IUCN Red List of Threatened Animals* published by the International Union for Conservation of Nature and Natural Resources (IUCN) and *Endangered and Threatened Wildlife and Plants* published in 1997 by the United States Government Printing Office (USGPO)

Extinct:	No sighting in the last 40 years
Endangered:	In danger of becoming extinct
Threatened:	A species that will become endangered if its present condition in the wild continues to deteriorate
Rare:	Not threatened, but not frequently found in the wild
In captivity:	A species that is extinct in the wild but has been kept successfully in captivity
Feral:	Animals that have been domesticated and have escaped into the wild
Common:	Frequently found within its range, which may be limited
Widespread:	Commonly found in many parts of the world

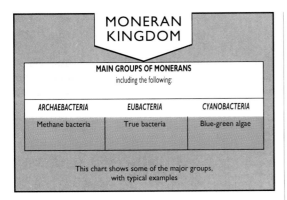

MONERAN KINGDOM

MAIN GROUPS OF MONERANS including the following:		
ARCHAEBACTERIA	EUBACTERIA	CYANOBACTERIA
Methane bacteria	True bacteria	Blue-green algae

This chart shows some of the major groups, with typical examples

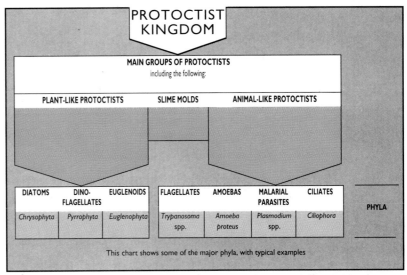

PROTOCTIST KINGDOM

MAIN GROUPS OF PROTOCTISTS including the following:							
PLANT-LIKE PROTOCTISTS			ANIMAL-LIKE PROTOCTISTS				
DIATOMS	DINO-FLAGELLATES	EUGLENOIDS	FLAGELLATES	AMOEBAS	MALARIAL PARASITES	CILIATES	PHYLA
Chrysophyta	Pyrrophyta	Euglenophyta	Trypanosoma spp.	Amoeba proteus	Plasmodium spp.	Ciliophora	

SLIME MOLDS

This chart shows some of the major phyla, with typical examples

Moneran, protoctist, and fungi kingdoms

Three groups of living things are not classified in the animal and plant kingdoms. These are the moneran, protoctist, and fungi kingdoms. Monerans are tiny, single-celled organisms that have no distinct nucleus. The nucleus is the control center of the cell. In contrast, protoctists and fungi have visibly distinct nuclei and tiny organs (called organelles). However, classification is a topic for much debate, and many scientists disagree on the classification of organisms in these three kingdoms.

The moneran kingdom contains all the microscopic, single-celled organisms that do not have distinct nuclei. The three main groups of monerans are: true bacteria, blue-green algae, and methane bacteria. The largest group of monerans is the true bacteria (*Eubacteria*).

For over a billion years, bacteria were the only living things on the earth. Then about 1.5 billion years ago, new organisms, called protoctists (formerly known as protists), evolved from the methane bacteria. All protoctists are single-celled organisms, but their cell structure is more complex than monerans. For example, protoctists have nuclei.

Scientists tend to classify an organism as a protoctist when they cannot place the organism in the animal, plant, or fungi kingdoms. Protoctists are grouped into phyla that have animal-, plant-, or fungus-like features. Single-celled algae, such as diatoms and euglenoids, behave like plants. Amoebas can move about and are more like animals. Slime molds form a subkingdom that have characteristics similar to the fungi kingdom.

Fungi make up the last kingdom of living things. Mushrooms, toadstools, and molds are all fungi. Fungi differ from animals and plants in that they depend on other organisms for their food. Like plants, fungi form groups called divisions. There are two divisions in the fungi kingdom.

See Volume 17 for more information on monerans, protoctists, and fungi.

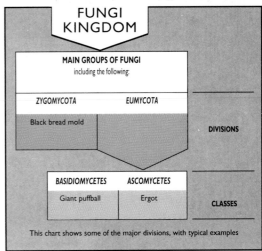

FUNGI KINGDOM

MAIN GROUPS OF FUNGI including the following:		
ZYGOMYCOTA	EUMYCOTA	DIVISIONS
Black bread mold		
BASIDIOMYCETES	ASCOMYCETES	CLASSES
Giant puffball	Ergot	

This chart shows some of the major divisions, with typical examples

COLOR GUIDE

MONERANS, PROTOCTISTS, & FUNGI

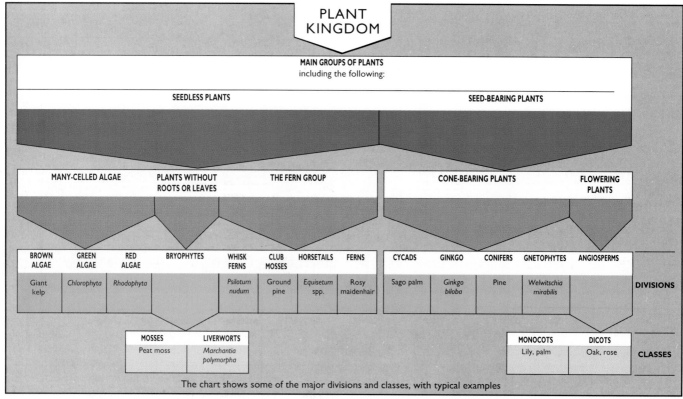

PLANT KINGDOM

MAIN GROUPS OF PLANTS
including the following:

SEEDLESS PLANTS	SEED-BEARING PLANTS

MANY-CELLED ALGAE	PLANTS WITHOUT ROOTS OR LEAVES	THE FERN GROUP	CONE-BEARING PLANTS	FLOWERING PLANTS

BROWN ALGAE	GREEN ALGAE	RED ALGAE	BRYOPHYTES	WHISK FERNS	CLUB MOSSES	HORSETAILS	FERNS	CYCADS	GINKGO	CONIFERS	GNETOPHYTES	ANGIOSPERMS	
Giant kelp	*Chlorophyta*	*Rhodophyta*		*Psilotum nudum*	Ground pine	*Equisetum* spp.	Rosy maidenhair	Sago palm	*Ginkgo biloba*	Pine	*Welwitschia mirabilis*		**DIVISIONS**

MOSSES	LIVERWORTS	MONOCOTS	DICOTS	
Peat moss	*Marchantia polymorpha*	Lily, palm	Oak, rose	**CLASSES**

The chart shows some of the major divisions and classes, with typical examples

The plant kingdom

Every plant, from the tiniest shrub to the tallest tree, belongs to the plant kingdom. There are about 500,000 different kinds (species) of plant that have been identified.

The plant kingdom (shown above) can be divided into 13 divisions. A plant division is similar to a phylum in animal classification. Each division represents a number of classes of plants that all have certain features in common.

The simplest plants are algae, all of which live in water. This set of books classifies three divisions of multicellular (or many-celled) algae in the plant kingdom. Some scientists, though, prefer to classify multicellular algae as protoctists.

Two classes, mosses and liverworts, make up the bryophyte division. These plants lack the roots, stems, and leaves that are found in other plant divisions.

The fern group comprises four divisions of the plant kingdom: whisk ferns, club mosses, horsetails, and ferns. All members of the fern group have two stages in their life cycle. During one of these stages tiny reproductive structures, called spores, are released. These spores will eventually grow into a new plant.

More complex plants reproduce with seeds. Four divisions of plants reproduce with "naked" seeds in cones. Cycads, conifers, ginkgoes, and gnetophytes are all cone-bearing plants.

Two classes, monocots and dicots, make up the largest division of plants, the angiosperms, or flowering plants. Unlike cone-bearing plants, angiosperms reproduce with enclosed seeds such as berries, nuts, and fruits.

See Volume 17 for more information on the different divisions of plants.

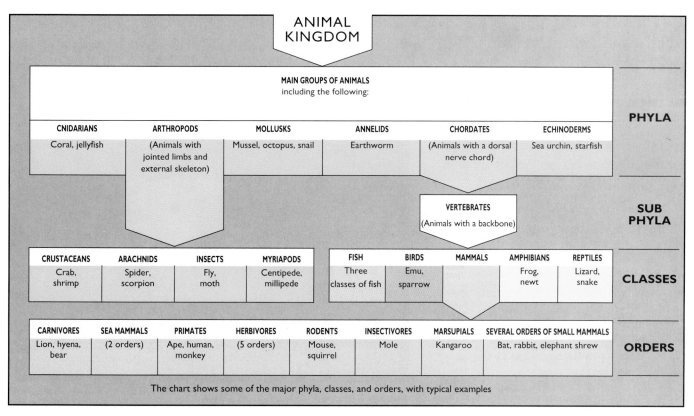

ANIMAL KINGDOM

MAIN GROUPS OF ANIMALS
including the following:

PHYLA

CNIDARIANS	ARTHROPODS	MOLLUSKS	ANNELIDS	CHORDATES	ECHINODERMS
Coral, jellyfish	(Animals with jointed limbs and external skeleton)	Mussel, octopus, snail	Earthworm	(Animals with a dorsal nerve chord)	Sea urchin, starfish

SUB PHYLA

VERTEBRATES
(Animals with a backbone)

CLASSES

CRUSTACEANS	ARACHNIDS	INSECTS	MYRIAPODS	FISH	BIRDS	MAMMALS	AMPHIBIANS	REPTILES
Crab, shrimp	Spider, scorpion	Fly, moth	Centipede, millipede	Three classes of fish	Emu, sparrow		Frog, newt	Lizard, snake

ORDERS

CARNIVORES	SEA MAMMALS	PRIMATES	HERBIVORES	RODENTS	INSECTIVORES	MARSUPIALS	SEVERAL ORDERS OF SMALL MAMMALS
Lion, hyena, bear	(2 orders)	Ape, human, monkey	(5 orders)	Mouse, squirrel	Mole	Kangaroo	Bat, rabbit, elephant shrew

The chart shows some of the major phyla, classes, and orders, with typical examples

The animal kingdom

In the eighteenth century, a botanist from Sweden named Carl von Linné (usually known by his Latin name, *Carolus Linneaus*) outlined a system of classifying plants and animals. This became the basis for classification all over the world. Scientists use Latin names so that all plants, animals, and other living things can be identified accurately, even though they have different common names in different places. Linneaus divided living organisms into two kingdoms: plants and animals. Today most scientists divide living things into five kingdoms: animals, plants, monerans, protoctists, and fungi. The animal kingdom (*above*) is divided into many phyla. Most of the phyla of the animal kingdom contain strange creatures – microscopic organisms, sponges, corals, slugs, and insects – without the backbone and central nervous system that we associate with more familiar animals.

Each phylum is divided into classes. For example, vertebrates (animals with a backbone) are a subdivision of a phylum and are divided up into seven classes: mammals, birds, reptiles, amphibians, and three classes of fish (represented by eels, sharks, and trout).

Each of these classes is broken down further into different orders. The mammal class, for instance, includes the orders carnivores (meat eaters), insectivores (insect eaters), primates (monkeys, apes), and marsupials (kangaroos, koalas), among others.

In this set of books, we give Latin names for different groups (genera) and kinds (species) of animals. See Volume 17 for more information on the different phyla of animals.

COLOR GUIDE

INVERTEBRATES

FISH

AMPHIBIANS & REPTILES

BIRDS

MAMMALS

PLANTS

BIOMES & HABITATS

MONERANS, PROTOCTISTS, & FUNGI

Opossum

Opossums are small, furry marsupials that are found in parts of North, Central, and South America. There are 77 species altogether, living in a wide range of habitats, from temperate forests through tropical forests, grasslands, mountains, and around human homes. Some live mainly on the ground, some mainly in trees, and there is even one species — the Yapok or Water opossum (*Chironectes minimus*) — that spends most of its time in the water.

The only species of opossum (and the only marsupial) found in North America is the Virginia opossum. This is the largest of the opossums; it is about the size of a domestic cat, although it is a little heavier and stockier, weighing about 12 lb (5.5 kg). It is a strange-looking creature, with large, naked ears and a long, hairless tail. Its face is long and pointed and whitish in color, with large, sensitive whiskers, although the rest of the body is covered with thick, dark underfur and white guard hairs.

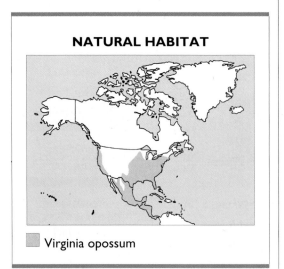

NATURAL HABITAT

Virginia opossum

Foraging through the garbage

The Virginia opossum has adapted well to human settlement, even foraging in garbage cans for food. It is what scientists call a generalist feeder, taking its food wherever it can find it. Unlike its tropical cousins, the woolly opossums and the Black-shouldered opossum, which only feed on fruit and nectar, the Virginia opossum feeds on a wide range of fruit, insects, small animals, and carrion (dead meat) such as that often found by the sides of busy highways.

The Virginia opossum is mainly active during the evening and nighttime and spends the day in a leafy nest built inside a rocky crevice, hollow tree, or another animal's abandoned burrow. Although it is mostly terrestrial (ground-dwelling), it is an expert climber, and prefers to center its home range around a woodland, often near water such as a small stream. When

▲ *This somewhat strange-looking animal is a Virginia opossum, photographed in Florida. Although it spends most of its time on the ground, it is well adapted to climbing trees, with hands and feet that can grip the branches firmly and a prehensile (grasping) tail.*

it does climb, it uses its hands and feet to grasp the branches, rather than using claws to get a good grip on the bark like many other tree-climbing animals. Its tail, too, is prehensile (able to grasp) and is so strong that it can hold onto a branch tightly and support the opossum's weight as it hangs upside down.

"Playing possum"

Generally a solitary animal, the Virginia opossum prefers to spend its time alone. It has a home range that may extend up to as much as 95 acres (40 hectares), although it does not appear to visit the entire area very often and does not show the defensive, territorial behavior of many other mammals. Each individual has several nest sites throughout its range – both on the ground and in trees – and travels between them, foraging for items of food as it goes.

If the opossum does encounter danger in its travels, it attempts to frighten off the rival or predator by hissing, growling, and screeching. However, if this does not work, it has a very neat defensive trick up its sleeve. It "plays possum," suddenly becoming totally limp and lifeless, with its eyes shut and mouth open, pretending to be dead and hoping that the animal will lose interest and go away. This trick is often very effective, and the opossum may remain in this state for less than a minute or to up to six hours!

Like other marsupials, opossums have a very short gestation period (the time when the babies are growing inside their mother) and give birth to extremely poorly developed young, which continue their development inside a special pouch on the mother's abdomen. In the case of the Virginia opossum, the offspring are born less than two weeks after mating.

These babies are tiny, but already have well-developed front legs with claws so that they can crawl to their mother's pouch. Once there, these claws drop off, and each baby clamps onto the nearest teat with its mouth, suckling milk in this way for the next three or four months.

There are usually 5-13 young, although a female may give birth to up to 56 in one litter! However, she only has a maximum of 13 teats in her pouch, so many baby opossums from such large litters die very shortly after they are born.

▲ *Unlike some of its more tropical cousins, the Virginia opossum does not restrict its diet to fruit and nectar. In this picture we can see the sharp teeth that are adapted to eating meat.*

KEY FACTS

● **Name**
Common or Virginia opossum (*Didelphis virginiana*)

● **Range**
North America from southern Canada, through central and eastern U.S. to northern Costa Rica; introduced into western U.S.

● **Habitat**
Woodlands, grasslands, around human habitation

● **Appearance**
A cat-sized animal, measuring 13-20 in (32.5-50 cm), with a long, bare tail of 10-21 in (25-53 cm); short legs with grasping feet, large, bare ears, and a long, pointed snout; thick, bushy fur that may be black, brown, or grayish-white

● **Food**
Fruit, insects, small animals, carrion, garbage

● **Breeding**
Female gives birth to 5-13 young that continue to grow in their mother's pouch for 2 months; adult at 3-4 months

● **Status**
Common

Orangutan

The orangutan is a large, fascinating primate, with striking red hair and long limbs for swinging through the trees. It belongs to a group of animals called the great apes, and it is closely related to chimpanzees and gorillas. Some 5000 years ago, the orangutan inhabited much of Asia, but today it is found in only a few areas on the Indonesian islands of Sumatra and Borneo. Here it lives in what remains of the lush rainforests that once covered much of these islands.

The tropical island rainforest occurs from low-lying areas to mountainous regions at altitudes of some 6000 ft (1828 m). Thick undergrowth covers the ground and the trees grow to heights of 150 ft (45.7 m). However, today most of the forest is being cleared to make way for rubber plantations and rice fields, or for the valuable timber that the trees provide. As a result, the orangutan's

habitat is disappearing at an alarming rate – and the orangutan with it.

Large apes

Male orangutans may reach up to $4\frac{1}{2}$ ft (1.37 m) when standing upright, and fully grown males may weigh as much as a man. The females are smaller: $3\frac{1}{2}$ ft (1.05 m) tall at the most and about half the weight of the males. Adult orangutans develop flabby areas of skin on the front of the neck known as laryngeal pouches; these grow to a large size in males and hang down over their chests. The males also grow mustaches and beards and have flanges (fatty swellings) on their cheeks.

With the possible exception of the gibbon, the orangutan is the most arboreal (tree dwelling) of the apes. It climbs swiftly and effortlessly, and travels with ease from branch to branch or tree to tree, usually by swinging from its arms

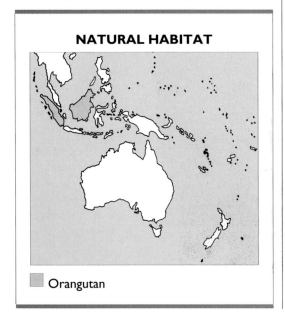

NATURAL HABITAT

Orangutan

▲ *The name orangutan is Malay and means "man of the forest." Like other apes, especially the chimp and gorilla, it has some characteristics that appear to be almost human. For example, it has four fingers and a short thumb that works like a human thumb, so that the ape can grasp objects, pick things up from the ground, and make small or fine movements. It also has an arched forehead and a very expressive face.*

but sometimes by walking along a branch like a tightrope walker. If a neighboring tree is just a little too far away, the orang shakes the tree he is in, swaying it from side to side until it reaches close enough for the ape to jump safely across.

Using "tools"

Some scientists have recorded occasions when an orangutan has grasped the branch or trunk of a neighboring tree with a hooked branch, so that it can bring the tree within its reach. Orangutans are also known to use other "tools." For example, although their coat is coarse and heavy, they frequently wait out a rainstorm under a large leaf that they have picked to use as an umbrella.

At night orangutans make leafy nests in trees, between 30-70 ft (9-21 m) from the ground. Each individual makes and uses its own nest, except for the young, who will sleep with their mother. Unlike chimps and gorillas, orangs are solitary apes that go about their daily life with very little contact with each other. Adult males and females come together to breed, and part immediately after mating.

Breeding can take place at any time of year, with a single young born nine months after the mother has mated. The baby orang weighs $3^1/_2$ lb (1.6-1.8 kg) and is only sparsely covered with hair on its back and head. It becomes physically adult at four years but does not breed until it is 10 years old. Females only breed every three to four years.

The orangutan is a gentle and appealing ape that appears to enjoy human company (although old males can become aggressive and dangerous). In Indonesia, orangutans were frequently captured and raised as pets or sent overseas to zoos, where they formed one of the main attractions. Scientists have estimated that attempts to capture just one young orangutan often resulted in the death of up to 10 others.

Efforts to conserve the orangutan in its natural habitat led to an agreement among all the zoos of the world that they would not take any more orangutans from their natural habitats in the wild. In Indonesia itself it is now illegal to sell, kill, or keep orangutans. The Indonesian government and international bodies are working to rehabilitate orangs kept as pets and return them to the wild in nature reserves set up in northern Sumatra.

◄ *This young orangutan, hanging from a branch, shows his long arms that are about $1^1/_2$ times as long as his legs.*

See also **Chimpanzee, Gorilla**

Orchid

About one in every ten flowering plants (angiosperms) on earth is an orchid. There are 400-800 groups (genera) of orchids and as many as 30,000 different kinds (species). Orchids relations include the amaryllis (family *Amaryllidaceae*) and the lily family (*Liliaceae*). One of the most economically valuable orchids to humans is *Vanilla planifolia,* the seed pods of which provide the vanilla used to flavor food and drink.

Habits and habitats

Orchids are found on every continent except Antarctica. They are especially common in the tropics. However, they do not grow in desert regions, because there is not enough moisture for them to grow. Orchids found in moderately cold (temperate) regions grow mainly in soil and have green, nonwoody stems; that is these plants are herbaceous.

▲ *This vanilla plant is artificially pollinated using a wooden needle.*

NATURAL HABITAT

Mexican vanilla

However, most orchids are found in the tropics, where they grow on other plants and trees. These orchids are epiphytes – plants that live on other plants without harming them. Most epiphytic orchids get the water and nutrients they need from organic (carbon-containing) material lodged in forks of trees and on rocks. The nutrients are absorbed through specially adapted roots. All epiphytic orchids have a spongy root covering called velamen that also enables them to absorb moisture from the surrounding air.

Other orchids are saprophytes; that is, they live off dead and rotting material. As with other saprophytic plants, these orchids generally live on the ground. They are usually small and herbaceous.

Orchid flowers

All orchid flowers are similar in structure, but there is a lot of variation in color and shape. One petal of each flower, called the lip, is often distinct in shape and color from the other petals. The lip forms at the top of the flower as the flower bud grows. As the flower matures, however, the stalk turns back

KEY FACTS

● **Name**
Mexican or
Bourbon vanilla
(*Vanilla planifolia*)

● **Range**
Native to Mexico and
Central and South
America; cultivated
worldwide in tropical
regions

● **Habitat**
Forests

● **Appearance**
Vine-like plant with
long, fleshy, climbing
stem; roots penetrate
soil; numerous
flowers open in
stages; each flower
lasts for about a day;
vanilla pod reaches
8 in (20 cm) in length
in 4 to 6 weeks,
taking up to 9 months
to fully mature

● **Life cycle**
Perennial

● **Uses**
Food flavorings

● **Status**
Common in
cultivation

on itself to bring the upper lip down into the lowest position. No one is quite sure why orchids do this.

While some orchids have small flowers – those of the genus *Pleurothallis,* for example, can be no more than ⅛ in (3 mm) across – others, including those from the genus *Cattleya,* have broad petals up to 9 in (23 cm) across. One species called *Brassia arcuigera* has long, thin petals that may measure as much as 18 in (45 cm) from tip to tip.

Unlike many flowers, the pollen of an orchid is not made up of tiny grains but is massed together into sticky balls (pollinia). These structures are carried from flower to flower by insects or birds, although some species sometimes self-pollinate.

The pollination of certain orchids is very complicated. Some use color and fragrant smells to attract insects and birds; others use nectar. In certain instances, orchids even mimic the shape of female insects to attract pollinating males.

Orchid seeds are tiny. The seed containers (capsules) of some species contain about three million dust-sized particles. These tiny, light particles are well adapted for dispersal by the wind. Each seed contains hardly any nutrients, and so orchids enlist the help of fungi to support them through germination.

Making vanilla

Commercial vanilla seed pods are the unripe fruit of the Mexican vanilla plant (*Vanilla planifolia*). This plant is native to Central and South America. Since it is such an economically valuable plant, however, it is cultivated worldwide in tropical regions.

The Mexican vanilla is a vine-like plant with a fleshy climbing stem. During the blooming season, its flowers open a few at a time, each lasting for about a day. In their natural habitat, the delicate flowers can be naturally pollinated only by a small Mexican bee; in other countries, laborers are hired to pollinate the plants artificially.

Following fertilization, the fruit or seed pod forms. The pod matures on the plant and is harvested. Curing is the process by which the active ingredient of the pod – vanillin – is allowed to develop. Thereafter, the pods are allowed four or five months to dry. The vanilla extract is prepared by crushing the cured, dried vanilla pods and extracting the tasty vanillin with alcohol.

► *The orchid* **Cattleya skinneri** *is the national flower of Costa Rica. This popular ornamental is now endangered due to overcollection in the wild.*

Oriole

▲ The nest of a Northern oriole is one of the most amazing nests found in the United States. Instead of resting it on a tree branch, the female oriole constructs an elaborate hanging pouch, woven from plant fibers and lined with soft materials. The male helps to feed the young on a diet of insects.

The orioles of North America (there are nine different species living here) are known for their glorious colors and songs. They are closely related to grackles and blackbirds, but they are not related to the European orioles. They have the same name because of their similar coloring: the name oriole comes from the Latin word *aureus*, meaning "golden."

The Northern oriole is a bird with very striking coloring, and one subspecies, the Baltimore oriole, was given its name because of its black and orange color. This coloring was similar to the flag of Lord Baltimore, founder of the state of Maryland. Until the 1970s, bird watchers thought that the Baltimore oriole was a different species to the Bullock's oriole that is found in the western part of North America. However, scientists now agree that these birds are both the same species, in spite of quite marked differences in their coloring.

Northern orioles live in fairly open woodland habitats such as orchards, parks, and gardens, or on the edge of denser woodlands, particularly near streams.

Engineering feats

Apart from its brilliant coloring, the Northern oriole is renowned for its skill in nest building. Each subspecies seems to show a preference for a particular type of tree, the western birds preferring natural woodlands, cottonwoods, and farmland, while the eastern orioles are more often found in backyards, where they seem to like elms, hickories, and oaks.

During the mating season, the male sings a loud and tuneful song. The female, with dull, brown coloring, is the nest builder. After mating, she chooses a suitable branch for the nest, often overhanging a road or stream, and works hard to get her nest built. She starts by hanging stems and grasses over the branch and then weaves more plant fibers, strings, and hairs in and out to create the circular rim of the nest. Next, she weaves a round pouch, usually from bark, yarn, and other material she finds. Finally, she lines the nest with softer materials. The whole process takes up to a

couple of weeks. Once it is finished, she lays her eggs. All the time she is at work, the male remains in the area, hunting for food and singing, almost as though he were encouraging his partner in her work.

The female lays her eggs in the depth of the nest. Usually there are four, but there may be up to six. The female Northern oriole sits on the eggs to keep them warm for up to two weeks. Once they have hatched they feed on insect larvae until

NATURAL HABITAT

Northern oriole

▲ *Northern orioles are often found near streams, where they settle on the banks to drink.*

they are old enough to take off. They learn to fly from the vantage point of a high perch: the nests are usually some 25-30 ft (8-10 m) above the ground.

After the breeding season, the male loses his bright feathers. At this time, the birds in the northern part of the range move southward. Some move as far south as South America in the winter months.

Fussy feeders

Although they are mainly insect eaters, the orioles of North America also take nectar from the cups of flowers. Because of their diet, it is difficult to attract orioles to garden bird feeders. However, some people have found that these birds have a sweet tooth, and if you hang half an orange in the garden you may be able to attract any Northern orioles that live in nearby woodlands.

See also **Blackbird, Oropendola**

Oropendola

Oropendolas belong to the same family as Red-winged blackbirds and Northern orioles. They are large, perching birds, found in the tropical countries of Central and South America. They love coffee and cocoa plantations, where tall trees have been grown to shade the farmed land, and they often choose to nest in lofty trees at the margins of the rainforest where land has been cleared for modern development. These habitats replace its natural choice, the tallest trees that tower over the dense growth of the tropical rainforests.

Oropendolas are much larger birds than their northern cousins, with stronger coloring. They have feathers in tones of black, rich chestnut brown, green, gold, and yellow, varying according to species. They are remarkable for their colonies of nests hanging from their favorite trees.

Nest weavers

The oropendolas live in large groups, with a handful of males sharing a territory with about 20 females. Sometimes there are as many as 100 birds in a colony. The females have a lot of work to do. At the start of the mating season, they weave a nest of long plant fibers taken from bananas, palms, or vines. They start by

KEY FACTS

- **Name**
Crested oropendola (*Psarocolius decumanus*)

- **Range**
Northern S. America

- **Habitat**
Treetops of humid forests

- **Appearance**
Up to 17 in (42 cm) long; a black head and body; a yellow and black tail; a large yellow bill

- **Food**
Invertebrates and small vertebrates; fruit; nectar

- **Breeding**
Small colonies, with more males than females; the females build elaborate hanging nests; 1 or 2 eggs, incubated for about 2 weeks

- **Status**
Common

◄ *The male Crested oropendola has dramatic glossy black coloring over his body that contrasts with the yellow tail and bill.*

wrapping some fibers around a twig, forming a loop at the bottom that will become the entrance to the nest. If they succeed in making a loop (and not all do!) they continue to weave plant material down from the loop to create a hanging sleeve. Finally they weave in more fibers to close the bottom of the nest.

After mating, the females add the finishing touch by lining their nests with dead leaves that will protect the eggs if the nest is buffeted by strong winds.

Food to hand

Oropendolas use their large, strong beaks to catch insects in the dense vegetation around and below their colonies. They also peck at the fruit of the trees and shrubs, and sometimes sip the nectar from some of the flowers. They are noisy and conspicuous birds, with little to fear in

NATURAL HABITAT

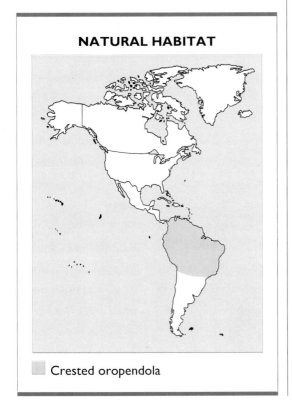

Crested oropendola

the treetops. However, some species of oropendola suffer from the invasion of a related species, the Giant cowbird. These parasitic birds lay their eggs in the nests of oropendolas, turning out the eggs of the host (the oropendola).

The different species occupy slightly different parts of the overall range. For example, Montezuma's oropendola, a large, rich brown bird, is found in Mexico and Panama, and the Green oropendola is found from Guyana across to Peru.

▲ *This colony of nests is typical of the oropendolas. They choose a tall, towering tree. The nests may be as much as 6 ft (2 m) long and take about ten days to build. While the females tend the eggs and the young, the males stand guard.*

See also **Blackbird, Oriole, Weaver bird**

Oryx

The oryx is a hardy antelope with a stocky body, long legs, and long, graceful horns. There are three species of oryx found in the Arabian and African deserts: the Arabian oryx, the gemsbok (or Beisa oryx), and the Scimitar-horned oryx.

All three species of oryx share one thing in common – the ability to survive in areas where few other antelopes even attempt to make a living. The oryx manages to survive in deserts – where temperatures can be both very hot and very cold – by adapting its body and behavior in various ways. These ways of adapting to the environment are best seen in the Arabian oryx, which is now extinct except for a single population that has been recently reintroduced to the Gulf State of Oman.

NATURAL HABITAT

◻ Gemsbok

In the summer months, when the temperature rises well above the animal's body temperature, the Arabian oryx adapts by growing a cooler, short-haired coat. The color of its markings lightens, too, becoming much paler to reflect the hot desert sun.

To cope with the high heat of summer days, the oryx rests in the shade from 8am to 6pm, and feeds throughout the night. In the winter, on the other hand, the animal combats the cold by developing a thicker coat and spends time in the morning resting in the sun to warm up.

Saving water

To survive in a desert, oryx must be able to go for long periods without water. Unlike some desert animals, oryx do need to drink, but once they do they can conserve water in a number of ways. In the summer, grazing at night and standing in the shade helps them to keep cool and save water. In addition, they have a very

▲ *Of the three species of oryx, the gemsbok is the most striking in appearance. The gray upperparts are separated from the white underparts by a black line running along the flanks, and it has conspicuous black and white markings on its face and legs. Both sexes are similar in color, and have long horns.*

▶ *Oryx live in dry, barren habitats, where water and vegetation are scarce. This herd of gemsbok are roaming the Namib Desert in southern Africa.*

efficient digestive system that allows them to urinate less frequently and makes their feces much drier. Finally, by getting up early and grazing on plants with dew on them, they manage to take in a reasonable amount of water even without drinking.

All three species of oryx share many features. Unlike most antelopes, both males and females have horns of a similar size – in fact, those of females are sometimes larger than those of males. The reason for this is unclear. Some scientists think that both sexes need these horns to protect themselves against common predators, and other scientists suspect that, in areas where resources are scarce, both sexes need to be able to compete fiercely for food.

The gemsbok and the true desert oryxes have different herding behavior, which reflects the environments in which they live. In the gemsbok, females live in small herds, males hold territories, and females travel to them to mate. However, Arabian and Scimitar-horned oryxes, which live in dry deserts where food is scarce, spend their time in mixed-sex herds. As soon a calf is born, the dominant male forms a consortship (bond) with the new mother, staying with her and her new calf for a day or two and mating with her almost immediately after she has given birth.

Reintroducing oryx to the wild

In the past, overhunting caused the Arabian oryx to become extinct in the wild. However, in recent years scientists have set up a large-scale reintroduction program in Oman and a smaller-scale program in Saudi Arabia. Such reintroductions give hope for the survival of animals which, while extinct in the wild, are represented in zoo collections around the world.

KEY FACTS

● **Name**
Gemsbok, Beisa oryx, or African oryx (*Oryx gazella*)

● **Range**
Parts of eastern and southern Africa

● **Habitat**
Dry areas

● **Appearance**
A heavy, stocky body, measuring up to 6 ft (1.8 m) in length and weighing up to 500 lb (225 kg); long legs, a long tail with a brush on the end; a large, rectangular face; 2 long, straight horns (the females' are longer and slimmer); distinctive black and white markings on its face and legs; gray upperparts and white underparts separated by a black line

● **Food**
Grass and leaves; can survive long periods without water

● **Breeding**
Females live in small herds, traveling to the males' territories after giving birth; 1 calf is born, between 8½ and 10 months after mating

● **Status**
Common

Osprey

The osprey's soaring flight and skill at hunting make it one of the most widespread birds in the world. Apart from the parts of the world that are too icy, too dry, or too mountainous, the only places where it is not found are New Zealand and Hawaii. Ospreys are a single species, divided into five subspecies.

NATURAL HABITAT

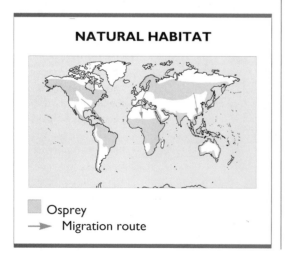

◻ Osprey
→ Migration route

▲ *This osprey has just caught a fish. You can see its strong legs. They are bare below the knee and its heavily feathered, muscular thighs look like trousers. Ospreys live mainly on fish, but they may catch small mammals, amphibians, invertebrates, or reptiles if they are forced to by lack of other food.*

The osprey is sometimes known as the Fish hawk, an apt description as it is closely related to the hawk, and is a specialized feeder, expert at fishing.

A fishing bird

The osprey flies with its wings held in a distinctive "M" shape. It can be seen circling over the water, sometimes as much as 230 ft (70 m) above the surface. Even from this height its sharp eyes can spot the glint of fish in the water. It dives for its prey with its wings held back and bent. It reaches its legs forward as it nears the water. Only its feet break the surface of the water as it dives for its catch, so its feathers do not get wet. Its toes, too, are adapted for catching fish. Each toe has a long, sharp talon, and the osprey can hold them so that two lie forward and two curve backward, giving it a firm grip on its slippery prey.

The osprey takes the fish back to a convenient perch – or its nest – to eat. As it flies off, it is often bullied and chased by competitors who may not have the same hunting skills: frigate birds are a particular menace in some parts of the world. In cooler zones, ospreys compete with Bald eagles (a type of fish eagle) for their prey.

Nests in the heights

Ospreys usually move to the northern parts of their range to breed. The male performs a dramatic courtship display, soaring high and diving at fantastic speed. He often carries a fish as a gift for his mate. Together, the birds build bulky nests, usually in trees, although they may choose rocky and inaccessible cliffs (a particular favorite with some of the European subspecies). If the pair are certain that there are no predators in the area, the nest may be built on the ground.

There are usually three eggs, and they are very striking, with red, brown, and cream mottled patterning. In the past these eggs were coveted by collectors, and in many places laws have been passed to protect the eggs. The eggs are closely guarded by the female.

Caring for the mother and young

The male brings food to his mate during the incubation period, which takes around five weeks. The male continues to feed the mother and young after the eggs have hatched, but as soon as the chicks are strong enough to be left on their own, the female joins the hunt for food for the chicks. In lean years, when there is not much food available, only the first of the chicks to hatch is likely to survive.

In the winter months, ospreys nesting in North America travel to Central and northern South America, and those in northern Eurasia move to Africa or India and Southeast Asia. You might be lucky enough to see one on its migration, resting at a lakeside or reservoir.

In most parts of the world, the osprey has been successful in hunting and breeding so that its numbers have remained steady. However, in Britain there has been a special problem with numbers. At the beginning of the twentieth century, ospreys were

overhunted by gamekeepers so that numbers dwindled. By the middle of the twentieth century, there were no ospreys at all in Britain. However, in the late 1950s, a pair came to Scotland and bird watchers set up a round-the-clock watch to insure their nest was not robbed. Gradually numbers have increased again.

In many parts of the world, ospreys have suffered from pesticide poisoning. Pesticides have filtered through farmlands into water and are absorbed by fish. Today strict controls on pesticide use mean that the birds are increasing in number again.

Although "osprey feathers" were very fashionable earlier in the twentieth century, these feathers were from egrets – relatives of the heron.

▼ *As it lands the osprey spreads its toes, which are unusual in that they are all the same length. The nest is large and untidy, usually in a tree.*

KEY FACTS

● **Name**
Osprey
(*Pandion haliaetus*)

● **Range**
Worldwide, apart from polar regions, deserts, and inland mountain ranges

● **Habitat**
Coasts, lakes, and rivers

● **Appearance**
22-23 in (55-58 cm); a brown back and wings with a white head, underside, and legs; the undersides of the wings and tail are mottled brown and white; a brown stripe through the eye and across the head; females are larger than males

● **Food**
Mainly fish

● **Breeding**
Large nest, lined with seaweed or other vegetation; swooping courtship flight; the female lays 3 eggs, incubated for 5 weeks; the male feeds the female; the young are born without feathers

● **Status**
Common in some regions, but rare in others; protected in many areas

Ostrich

Ostriches are superlative creatures: the heaviest birds, the fastest birds, and the tallest birds. And they are flightless. They can run across the open grasslands of

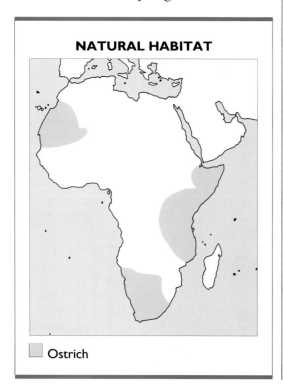

NATURAL HABITAT

☐ Ostrich

eastern and southern Africa at the speed of a horse – over 30 mph (50 km/h). This speed has enabled them to survive in spite of the stealthy hunters that share their habitat, including big cats such as lions, leopards, and cheetahs.

Male ostriches are mainly black, with showy white feathers on their flightless wings and tails. The females have a much more subtle coloring of earthy brown that blends with the landscape. There are four subspecies of ostrich, with slightly different skin colors, found in different parts of Africa. A fifth subspecies, the Arabian ostrich, became extinct in the wild early in the twentieth century.

Traveling birds

The birds need to be able to travel fast and far in search of food in the semideserts where they live. They "graze" on the plants they can find, eating shoots,

▲ *These male ostriches, with their stark black and white coloring, are conspicuous but are able to escape danger by running at high speed.*

▶ *Young ostriches have sandy brown coloring to disguise them in their sandy habitat. Their feathers are spiky to make them less appetizing to predators. They grow rapidly, reaching full height in a year; however, less than a quarter of the young flock survive.*

leaves, flowers, and seeds. They lower their heads to eat, but keep lifting their heads to scan the horizon for predators. If they do meet an attacker at close quarters, they kick, clawing downward with their strong front claws.

As they peck at the plants around, they collect the food in their gullets, rolling it into what is known as a bolus. Every now and again they swallow the bolus in one large gulp. You can see the lump of food going down an ostrich's neck.

Shared childcare

Ostriches usually live in loose flocks, with a single male and several females. One female is the dominant one. The male stakes out a territory, providing a selection of nestings sites – scraped out hollows. He displays to the female by squatting down, fanning out his feathers and waving each wing at her in turn. The leading female selects one of these hollows and lays up to a dozen eggs in two weeks.

Other females may also lay eggs in the same nest. The eggs, as you would expect from the biggest birds, are the largest of all birds' eggs. They are popular with local people – a single egg provides an omelet for 15 people! Although they are big, these eggs are not large in relation to the size of the parents. This means that the parents can cover a large number of eggs at one time when incubating them.

The male and leading female guard the eggs closely; usually, the female sits on the eggs by day, well disguised by her dull brown feathers. The male stands guard and keeps predators away with aggressive displays, fanning out his wing feathers and strutting up and down, ready to attack with his sharp, heavy claws. At night the male takes over nest duties.

After hatching, the young look rather like balls of feathers on stilts! They are soon on the move. Several broods usually join together in a flock, running with their parents in search of food.

KEY FACTS

● **Name**
Ostrich
(*Struthio camelus*);
four subspecies

● **Range**
Southern Sahara
across to the Horn
of Africa, eastern and
southern Africa

● **Habitat**
Arid grasslands and
scrub

● **Appearance**
7 ft 6 in (2.5 m) tall;
males are black with
white feathers on the
wings and tail; a bare
neck and thighs; the
female is muddy
brown; skin color
varies according to
subspecies; two toes;
the young are well-
camouflaged

● **Food**
Vegetation

● **Breeding**
The male performs
an elaborate display;
12 eggs are laid and
incubated by both
birds for over 40
days; the young run
together in a flock
with their parents

● **Status**
The North African
subspecies is
endangered; the
Arabian subspecies
is endangered and
extinct in the wild

Otter

Otters are the water lovers of the weasel family. They are sleek, streamlined animals, with long and slender but muscular bodies, relatively long tails, and short, powerful legs. They share this characteristic shape with other members of the weasel family such as mink, ferrets, and polecats.

A giant cousin

Most otters live in freshwater rivers and lakes. They include the Giant otter (*Pteronura brasiliensis*), three species of clawless otters, and eight species of river otters. In North America, for example, the North American river otter (*Lutra canadensis*) is found on inland waterways and estuaries throughout Alaska, Canada, and parts of the northern United States. Otters are strong swimmers, hunting underwater for their favorite foods, frogs, fish, crabs, and so on. The largest (and rarest) otter is the Giant otter, which may grow up to 6 ft (2 m) from head to tail and weigh as much as 66 lb (30 kg).

The Sea otter, however, is a saltwater mammal. It is found around the North Pacific, all along the west coast of North America and the Asian coast of the Bering Sea. Unlike most otters, it spends almost all of its time in the water, only venturing out occasionally to rest on rocks. As a result, its body is extremely well adapted to swimming, with webbed hind feet and a thick, but sleek, waterproof coat – so much so that it is very awkward on land and cannot walk very quickly or easily.

A laid-back attitude

The Sea otter is generally diurnal (active during the day) and sleeps in the water at night. It lies on its back to do this, often in the middle of a kelp bed (a mass of seaweed) with some of the fronds wrapped around it to stop it drifting away. Sometimes it sleeps with one of its forepaws covering its eyes. During the day it spends its time in the rocky coastal shallows, hunting and diving for food on its own or resting in small groups.

The Sea otter's diet is made up of small fish, crustaceans, or mollusks, of which it needs to eat 20-25 percent of its body weight a day to survive. It finds these by diving below the surface of the water for up to five minutes at a time, foraging on the ocean floor or among the thick beds of kelp. Along with some primates, the Sea otter is one of the few mammals to use tools, and it has been known to

► *These Sea otters off the coast of Alaska are resting in the water. They make sure that they do not drift away on the tide by lying on their backs and wrapping seaweed fronds around them.*

▼ *Otters are expert underwater swimmers. The North American river otter is found mainly in freshwater habitats. It has a layer of waterproof fur with a softer layer beneath. Its long whiskers are very sensitive, helping it to "feel" for its prey in murky water.*

- **Name**
  Sea otter
  (*Enhydra lutris*)

- **Range**
  North Pacific Ocean

- **Habitat**
  Coastal waters

- **Appearance**
  A long, streamlined body measuring 39-47 in (1-1.2 m), with a tail of 10-14 in (25-37 cm); sleek, waterproof fur; the upperparts vary in color from reddish-brown through dark brown and black; the underparts and head are gray or creamy; short legs with webbed hind feet

- **Food**
  Slow-moving fish, crustaceans, mollusks

- **Breeding**
  Female gives birth to 1 (sometimes 2) offspring at sea; the pup is well developed and active within a day; its mother swims on her back and the pup suckles, lying on her chest, until it can swim at around 2 weeks

- **Status**
  One subspecies, the Southern sea otter (*Enhydra lutris nereis*), is threatened

dislodge mollusks such as abalone from rocks by banging on the edge of the shells with a large stone or piece of rock.

Unlike river otters, the Sea otter catches its prey in its forepaws rather than its jaws and carries it to the surface of the water. Here, the otter lies on its back, using its chest as a kind of "lunch counter." Soft food such as fish can be held in the forepaws and eaten as it is, but mollusks need a little more work! The otter places the tightly closed shell on his chest and hammers it repeatedly with a small rock that he has brought up from the seabed until it breaks and he can get to the soft, tasty insides.

NATURAL HABITAT

☐ Sea otter

Valuable fur

Life can get cold in the water, especially during the winter. However, unlike most sea mammals, the Sea otter does not have an extra layer of fat to keep it warm. Instead, it relies on the protection of its two layers of fur: a long, thick layer of underfur and a covering of waterproof hairs. Air trapped within these hairs helps to keep the animal warm.

Of all mammals, the Sea otter's fur is possibly the most valuable to the fur industry, and Sea otters were almost hunted to extinction during the early twentieth century. However, they have been protected since 1911, and populations have increased and become more widespread since then.

The biggest danger for the Sea otter today is accidental death – either from drowning in modern fishing nets or from the devastating effects of oil pollution. It is estimated that at least 6000 of these vulnerable creatures were killed when the oil tanker *Exxon Valdez* was wrecked on Prince William Sound off the coast of Alaska in 1989.

See also **Kelp and other seaweeds, Ocean**

Owl

KEY FACTS

- **Name**
  Barn owl (*Tyto alba*)

- **Range**
  35 subspecies found worldwide except Canada, Eurasia, the Sahara, Antarctica

- **Habitat**
  Woodlands and farmlands

- **Appearance**
  13-14 in (33-36 cm) long; a pale white breast and face; a golden head, back, and wings; a large, heart-shaped face; a short beak; short legs with sharp talons

- **Food**
  Small mammals, reptiles, amphibians, and invertebrates

- **Breeding**
  2-3 eggs are laid a couple of days apart; incubated for just over a month; the female incubates the eggs while the male forages

- **Status**
  Widespread

While eagles, hawks, and related species are masters of the air during the day, owls take over at night. With their large, round faces, forward-facing eyes, and feathered ears, they are quite unlike any other group of birds.

Owls are perfectly adapted to hunting at night. Their forward-facing eyes allow them to scan the ground for movement; their eyes are also large so they can pick up as much detail as possible.

Sound advantage

Buried beneath their feathers, many species of owl have large ears that are arranged asymmetrically, with one above and behind the eye and the other level with the beak. This arrangement means that they can hear their prey and judge how far away it is. The circular arrangement of feathers around the eyes is thought to help with their hearing. The feathers pick up and direct sounds, rather like a satellite dish picking up signals.

In experiments, Barn owls have been able to catch prey in complete darkness, directed only by their ears. And the Great gray owl (*Strix nebulosa*) has been seen catching small mammals buried in the

NATURAL HABITAT

Barn owl

snow, again using only its power of hearing to direct it. The owl looks as if it has no neck at all, but in fact its neck is very long and flexible, buried beneath the thick feathers around its ears. It can actually turn its head a full 180 degrees so it can see behind itself.

The downy feathers of an owl give it a silent flight that serves two purposes. The owl is less likely to disturb its prey, and it is more likely to be able to hear any creatures moving around so that it can follow them, waiting to go in for the kill.

Keen hunters

Although most owls hunt at dusk or dawn, some always hunt in the day. Indeed, many species come out during the day, but they have to protect their eyes with what is known as a third eyelid (a nictitating membrane). This is translucent, allowing some light through but not too much. (Another bird that uses its third eyelid to protect its eyes is the grebe. It covers its eyes as it dives under water.)

The main prey of owls is small animals; the exact species they catch vary widely according to the owls's habitat. For example, the Great horned owl has been known to catch waterfowl such as duck and geese, but it also chases skunks, rats, and other farm pests. The Barn owl goes for smaller prey, particularly voles and mice, but also rats. Pygmy owls from North and South America and Africa feed on lizards, young birds, and insects. It seems that anything small that moves in an owl's territory is at risk.

Owls have light bodies relative to the size of their wings. This means that they can fly effortlessly and with great control, but they are not renowned for their speed. They start their hunt by perching on a fence or tree, checking out the land. Here, their ability to turn their head is important: because their eyes are forward facing, they can only see directly in front of them. As they watch and wait for prey, they turn their heads with sudden, silent

▼ *At dusk, Barn owls start to hunt, catching voles, mice, and rats for themselves and their young. This owl is using a post as a lookout point, and turns its head to scan the ground for its prey.*

▲ *This Great gray owl has very acute hearing that is improved by the arrangement of its feathers. The circular "dishes" around its eyes help to direct the sounds toward its ears. The small, hooked beak is almost covered by the feathers.*

and controlled jerks, blinking and refocusing in an instant. Some owls prefer to scan the territory from the air, flying low and slowly along rivers, streams, or roads with their eyes on the ground.

Once they spot their prey they swoop silently and grab it in their sharp claws. Then they transfer it to their small hooked beaks, which are sometimes almost buried in feathers. They carry small prey back to a perch to swallow it whole.

Owls (and most other birds of prey) have complex digestive systems. Because they do not pick at their food or chew it, all the indigestible material (fur, bones, and so on) is swallowed with the meal. In the digestive tract these parts are separated out and formed into a sausage-shaped pellet, with the bony parts of the prey wrapped in fur. This makes it easier for the owl to bring it back into its mouth and spit it out. Scientists use these pellets to see whether owls are living in an area and to find out what they eat.

Different groups

Scientists divide owls into two groups: the typical owls, and the Barn and bay owls. There are well over a hundred species of typical owl and more are being found all the time. They are difficult to identify in remote areas because they often come out only at night. Typical owls include eared and horned owls, eagle owls, Snowy owls, and Tawny owls. This group also includes the smallest owls, the pygmy owls of South America (the Least pygmy owl, at 4½ in [12 cm] is the smallest). There are also fish owls that specialize in catching fish. Eagle owls, on the other hand, hunt mainly birds, often catching them in midair. The Barn and bay owls are a much smaller group of owls, with distinctive heart-shaped faces.

The familiar hooting call of many owls is made for two reasons. The male calls to ward off rivals that might be thinking of entering his territory, and both male and female call to each other to keep in touch while hunting. The Barn owl does not hoot, and the ten species that make up the group of Barn and bay owls make hissing, screeching, or whistling noises.

Owls are good judges of the amount of prey in an area, and they seem to be able to adjust their breeding habits accordingly. In years where there are plenty of small mammals, for example, owls in the area tend to mate early in the year and raise several broods. Like many other birds of prey, they lay two to three eggs at intervals of two to three days. All three chicks only survive in years when there is plenty of food.

Breeding and protection

Owls usually find convenient holes in trees or rocky outcrops for their nests. Some large species that cannot find suitable holes may take over the nests of other birds such as crows or other birds of prey. Some owls that live in open grasslands lay their eggs in hollows on the ground. Burrowing owls may actually dig

NATURAL HABITAT

Great horned owl

a burrow, although they usually take over the tunnels of prairie dogs.

Until recently, owls were generally disliked and heavily persecuted. They are also the subject of many superstitions and romantic stories. However, the idea of an owl as a wise bird is closer to the truth. Owls are very skillful and serve a useful role in controlling pests and maintaining the natural balance in many different habitats. In some cases, owls captured from the wild have been easy to tame, showing that they are intelligent.

A handful of the 140 or more identified owls are threatened or endangered: these include the Spotted owl (*Strix occidentalis*) of northwestern United States and several tropical species, including the Anjouan scops owl (*Otus rutilus capnodes*) and the Giant scops owl (*Otis gurneyi*).

◀ *The Great horned owl is a typical owl, mainly brown in color. Its prominent "horns" are tufts of feathers.*

KEY FACTS

● **Name**
Great horned owl (*Bubo virginianus*)

● **Range**
N. America, apart from the far north, south to southern Chile (excluding the West Indies)

● **Habitat**
Woodlands, farmlands, parklands, mountainous regions

● **Appearance**
Large owl, up to 23 in (58 cm); tones of reddish- and golden brown, with mottled and streaked effect; a reddish facial disk; yellow eyes; "horns" of dark feathers

● **Food**
Small mammals

● **Breeding**
Builds nest in a hole; 2-3 eggs are laid a couple of days apart and incubated by the females for just over a month; the males forage for food

● **Status**
Widespread

See also **Eagle, Grebe, Hawk, Osprey, Prairie dog**

Oxpecker

◄ *These Yellow-billed oxpeckers "groom" an African buffalo.*

KEY FACTS

● **Name**
Yellow-billed oxpecker (*Buphagus erythrorhynchus*)

● **Range**
Africa south of Sahara

● **Habitat**
Grasslands and farmland where cattle graze

● **Appearance**
7-9 in (18-23 cm) long; a yellow bill with a red tip; dark gray-brown above with a gray-brown chest and chin; paler underparts and tail

● **Food**
Insects and animal tissue

● **Breeding**
Nest of grass, feathers, and hair in a hole in a tree, bank, or building; 2-3 eggs, incubated by both parents; adult helpers assist the parents

● **Status**
Rare apart from animal reserves

NATURAL HABITAT

Yellow-billed oxpecker

Oxpeckers are members of the starling family. They get their name from their feeding habits: they sit on the backs of cattle and feed on the ticks buried in their skin. This behavior is met with mixed feelings by the people in the parts of Africa where they live.

Local tribespeople appreciate the work of the oxpeckers in keeping their cattle clear of ticks. Commercial farmers, with larger herds in smaller areas, claim that the oxpeckers also harm their animals by keeping the wounds open and feeding on blood and animal tissue; they also suspect the oxpeckers of carrying disease from one member of the herd to another. Hunters — both human and nonhuman — dislike the oxpeckers because they are wary birds that take off with a noisy alarm call if they sense predators in the area, warning their hosts to take cover as well.

Many of the oxpeckers' hosts do not seem to mind the activities of these small parasitic birds — they just continue to graze with a small flock of oxpeckers on their backs.

Out on the grasslands

There are two species of oxpecker. The Yellow-billed oxpecker was originally found all over Africa south of the Sahara. The Red-billed oxpecker had a more limited range in eastern and southern Africa. They spend most of their waking hours clinging to the backs of large mammals. These include antelope, cattle, giraffes, rhinos, and hippos.

Oxpeckers have flattened bills, which they use to comb the animals' hides for ticks and bloodsucking flies. Although their main nourishment comes from the blood-filled insects, they also feed on blood from the wounds and may peck at the tissues around the wounds.

Even their courtship display is performed on the backs of their hosts. They build their nests in holes or under the eaves of traditional buildings and line them with the hairs of their hosts.

Pesticides used to control parasitic insects among cattle have poisoned and virtually eliminated oxpeckers throughout their natural habitat, so that they are now only found in nature reserves.

▶ *This Red-billed oxpecker on the back of a giraffe, uses its stiff tail to prop itself up. Its strong, curved claws grip onto the animal's hide.*

Palm

The distinctive shape of the palm tree immediately conjures thoughts of some tropical island. As well as having a striking physical appearance, palms are extremely important to humans. They are important building materials and sources of fibers, food, fuel, oils, waxes, and even wine.

Altogether, there are about 2800 species of palm tree in the family *Palmae*. They typically have thin, straight, unbranched trunks about 3 ft (1 m) across. Palm trees may be tall, occasionally reaching heights of 200 ft (60 m). Their leaves, which sprout from the top of the tree and hang downward, have long stalks and are fan- or feather-shaped. The leaf size varies greatly, from several inches upward. At more than 65 ft (20 m) long, the leaves of the Raffia palm (*Raphia ruffia*) are the largest in the plant kingdom.

Ancient plants

Palms are one of the oldest flowering plants (angiosperms). Fossil hunters have discovered the remains of palms in rocks dating from the Triassic Period, over 200 million years ago. Today palm trees are a common sight in the tropics. There are nearly 1400 species in Asia and more than 1100 species in tropical America, especially Brazil, which alone has more than 500 species. Just over 100 species are native to Africa.

Although they are mainly tropical plants, some palm species thrive in cooler environments. For example, the Windmill palm (*Trachycarpus fortunei*) is native to eastern Asia but may be cultivated outdoors in temperate climates as far north as Vancouver in Canada. Another hardy species is the Needle palm (*Rhapidophyllum hystrix*) of the southeastern

KEY FACTS

● **Name**
Date palm
(*Phoenix dactylifera*)

● **Range**
Middle East and North Africa

● **Habitat**
Dry regions

● **Appearance**
Thin, straight, unbranched trunk grows to 75 ft (25 m), ending with a crown of shining leaves about 16 ft (5 m) long; male and female flowers grow on separate trees; fruits (dates) one seeded and vary in color, shape, and size; up to 1000 dates may grow on a single tree

● **Life cycle**
Perennial

● **Uses**
Fibers; food and drink; fuel; timber

● **Status**
Widespread in the wild; common in cultivation

◄ *Date palms (Phoenix dactylifera) grow in a plantation in the Middle East.*

United States, which can survive temperatures as low as -6°F (-21°C).

Palm structure

Palm flowers are usually small and may appear singly, in pairs, in threes, or in large clusters called inflorescences. Protective structures called bracts surround the young inflorescences and allow them to mature without interference from animals or insects.

The fruits of palms can be berries, drupes, or nuts, depending on the shape of a female reproductive structure called the ovary. The fruit of the Coconut palm (*Cocos nucifera*) has an outer husk and is called a drupe.

Not all palms are tall, erect trees. Some, such as the Needle palm, have creeping, vine-like stems, while the stems of species from the group (genus) *Nypa* are completely hidden underground.

NATURAL HABITAT

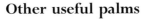

■ Date palm

Other palms are shrub-like plants.

The Date palm

The Date palm (*Phoenix dactylifera*) has been cultivated throughout the Middle East for thousands of years. This popular ornamental tree is very important to humans. Like its relative, the Coconut palm (*Cocos nucifera*), all parts of the tree are used to make valuable products. The trunk is used for timber, the leaves to make baskets and for fuel, and the fruits are a popular food in many countries.

Other useful palms

Palms are an extremely important group of plants to humans. Many species are cultivated for a variety of different uses. For example, the Asian sugar palm (*Arenga pinnata*) is an important source of sugar. The sap is tapped from the bracts surrounding the flowers and is used to make palm wine and a liquor called arrack. Similar drinks may also be obtained from the sap of the Toddy palm (*Caryota urens*) and the Coconut palm.

Cabbage palmeto (*Sabal palmetto*) from the southeastern United States and the Caribbean has a water-resistant trunk, so the timber is used to make piers and jetties. Like the Date palm, Cabbage palmeto is also a popular ornamental tree.

▲ *A Date palm bearing fruits. The trees start to bear fruits after four or five years growth, reaching maximum fruit production after about 15 years. Egypt, Iran, Iraq, and Saudi Arabia are the leading date-exporting countries, although the trees are grown for fruit in many other countries.*

See also **Coconut palm**

Panda

There are two species of animal called the panda: the large black and white, bear-like Giant panda, and the smaller Lesser, or Red panda (also called the Cat bear), which looks like a raccoon. The Red panda occurs across a fairly large area, from southern China to northern Burma.

▼ *The Giant panda eats mainly bamboo, but its body is not able to digest it efficiently and so it has to eat for about 10-12 hours a day just to survive!*

The Giant Panda lives only in the bamboo forests that grow in the mountains of the Szechwan province in southwestern China.

A rare and unusual mammal

Little is known about the Giant panda, mainly because it is very shy and secretive and lives in places that are almost inaccessible. It inhabits the cold, damp ravines and clifftops of bamboo forests, which occur at altitudes of about 5000-10,000 ft (1524-3048 m). It lives alone, except when breeding, and spends most of its time moving slowly over the ground, although it will climb trees if necessary.

Scientists classify the Giant panda as a carnivore, but its main food is bamboo, and pandas kept in captivity have managed to survive eating only this plant. In the wild, however, the Giant panda sometimes supplements its diet with other plants such as crocuses, and animals such as birds, small rodents, and fish, which it catches by flipping them out of the water.

The animal has adaptations for eating bamboo that are not found in any other mammal. First, it has a long wrist bone in its foreleg, which is covered with a fleshy pad. This forms a sixth digit, a kind of "thumb" that, along with the other five digits, makes it easier for the Giant panda to grasp bamboo stems.

Second, the Giant panda has huge teeth called molars, with ridges and bumps for crushing the bamboo stems (culms). And third, it has strong facial muscles for chewing the tough plant fibers.

KEY FACTS

● **Name**
Giant panda
(*Ailuropoda
melanoleuca*)

● **Range**
Western China

● **Habitat**
Bamboo forest

● **Appearance**
A large, robust body,
about 6 ft (1.8 m)
long, with a short,
stubby tail; a thick,
dense white coat
with black legs, ears,
and shoulders, and
distinctive black
markings around the
eyes; a fully grown
adult weighs about
300 lb (136 kg)

● **Food**
Mainly bamboo
shoots and stems;
also other plants and
small birds, rodents,
and fish

● **Breeding**
1-2 young born at a
time in a sheltered
den, 4-5 months
after mating; the cubs
are blind and helpless
at birth and only
weigh 3-4 $^{1}/_{2}$ oz
(90-120 g); they are
suckled until about
6 months old and
become independent
at about a year old

● **Status**
Endangered

In the winter, the Giant panda goes about its daily life among ice and snow. It is well insulated from the cold by its thick coat; fur on the soles of its hind feet not only keeps out the cold, but helps the feet grip on slippery surfaces.

A relative newcomer

The Giant panda's bamboo forests are extremely difficult places for outsiders to get to as well as travel through. For centuries the local people knew of the Giant panda's existence and had hunted it, but it was unknown to the western world until 1869 when it was first seen by a European, the famous French missionary and naturalist Père David. The first Giant panda to be seen by the general public was one that was brought to the Chicago zoo in 1936. Since that time the Chinese government has donated Giant pandas to other zoos, notably in Washington D.C., Mexico, and London. Efforts to breed the Giant panda in captivity have so far yielded favorable results only in China.

Père David's "discovery" of the Giant panda presented scientists with a problem. What kind of animal was it, a bear or a raccoon? Although the Giant panda looks like a bear, its reproductive organs and scent glands are similar to those of animals in the raccoon family. Finally, after years of argument, it was agreed that the Giant panda really belonged with the bears. The Red panda, however, is still classified as a type of raccoon.

The Giant panda is one of the world's rarest animals. Scientists believe that only a small number of these unusual mammals are left in the wild and that the panda is

▲ *A symbol for the World Wildlife Fund, the
Giant panda is one of the most familiar animals
in the world, with its large "cuddly" body and
distinctive black and white coloring.*

on the very brink of extinction. This may be for several reasons, including their low reproduction rate. One of the main problems, however, is that the Giant panda relies so heavily on bamboo, which its body is unable to digest efficiently. Efforts to save the Giant panda have mostly been unsuccessful.

NATURAL HABITAT

▢ Giant panda

See also **Bamboo**

Pangolin

The pangolin is a unique and highly specialized mammal that lives almost exclusively on ants and termites. It is found in parts of Africa and Asia and is the Old World equivalent of the South American anteater.

One of the main features that distinguishes mammals from other animals is the hairy covering on their bodies. In some mammals, however, only small traces of this characteristic remain – in the whiskers of the naked mole rat, for example. In a few other mammals this hair has been modified (converted) into another material. For example, the armadillo's body is protected by bony plates covered with horn, and the pangolin is distinguished from all other mammals by its covering of hard scales.

NATURAL HABITAT

☐ Cape pangolin

A scaly anteater

Almost the entire surface of the pangolin's body is protected by these scales. They extend over the top of the head, the back, along the upper parts of the forelegs and hind legs, and over all surfaces of the tail. The underbelly and the underparts of the limbs are soft and hairy and, when in danger, the pangolin rolls itself up into a spiral so that only the scaly parts of the body are exposed on the outside. (The name pangolin comes from a Malayan word meaning "the roller.") This gives the creature protection from predators.

The pangolin has become remarkably adapted to a life spent largely among ants and termites. Its scales protect it from the stings of its prey, as do the thick eyelids that shield its small eyes. It does not have external ears and it can close its nostrils while it is feeding as a defense against swarming insects. It scoops up termites and ants by extending its extremely long

▲ *Pangolins are strange-looking mammals, with small, pointed heads, long, broad tails, and large, rounded bodies covered with scales. In many species, these scales are sharply pointed, but those of the Cape pangolin (shown above) have wide, rounded edges, and they overlap each other like tiles on a roof.*

tongue, which is covered with a sticky mucus. In some species the tongue can be extended for about 12 in (30 cm) although its total length is much longer than this. The tongue is actually anchored in the animal's pelvic area, in the lower part of its abdomen.

The pangolin's body is long, as is the tail. The head is narrow with a pointed snout and a small mouth. The animal has no need for teeth, so the jaws are toothless. Each of its limbs has five digits that end in sharp claws. On the forelegs, the middle three claws are longer and are used for digging.

Pangolins move about rather slowly on the ground, walking on the sides or knuckles of the forelegs; the long claws prevent the animal from placing the foot flat on the ground. From time to time pangolins may walk on their hind legs with their body half erect and their forelegs in the air. This is also the stance they adopt when attacking a termite nest.

On the ground or in the trees?

There are seven species of pangolin, four of which are found in Africa (the Giant, Cape, Small-scaled tree, and Long-tailed pangolins) and three of which are found in Asia (the Indian, Chinese, and Malayan pangolins). The Small-scaled tree and Long-tailed pangolins are the smallest of the African species, and both spend most of their time in trees. The Long-tailed pangolin lives mainly in the forest canopy where it feeds on tree ants.

The Giant pangolin is the largest of the seven species; its head and body measurements may be up to 30 in

(75 cm), with a slightly shorter tail. Both the Giant and the Cape pangolins are ground-dwelling animals that occupy burrows while they are resting and when giving birth. All of the Asian species live on the ground, although they can climb trees if necessary. These species are distinguished from their African relatives by having hair at the base of each scale.

Persecuted by humans

In Africa, the local people kill pangolins for their edible flesh and for their scales, which are used for decorative objects and as lucky charms. Local people in both Asia and Africa believe that the scales can be used in medicines and many pangolins are also killed for this reason. All species are threatened as a result, with the Cape pangolin particularly endangered.

▲ *Although mainly a ground-dwelling species, this Malayan pangolin may climb trees to escape from predators. This one is rolled up into a ball and hanging by its prehensile (grasping) tail.*

KEY FACTS

● **Name**
Cape or Temmincks ground pangolin (*Manis temmincki*)

● **Range**
Eastern, central, and parts of southern Africa

● **Habitat**
Dry regions where there is little vegetation and light, sandy soil

● **Appearance**
A large, squat body, measuring about 20 in (50 cm) with a slightly shorter tail of about 14 in (35 cm); the body is covered in large, rounded scales that overlap; the head is small and pointed, with tiny ears

● **Food**
Ants and termites

● **Breeding**
A single offspring, weighing 10-14 oz (300-400 g), is born about 5 months after mating; it is carried around on its mother's tail at first; its mother suckles it for about 3 months, although it can begin to eat solid food at around 1 month old

● **Status**
Endangered

See also **Armadillo**

Parrot

Brightly colored, usually forest green, often with a flash of exotic red or yellow, with chunky seed-eating bills, the 260 species of parrots, parakeets, and lovebirds in the family *Psittacidae* are easily recognized by almost everyone. Found in the tropical regions of Africa, Asia, Australia, and South America, parrots and their relatives are most common in the rainforests of South America and Australasia. However, some species from Australia, including the budgerigar, live on the open plains.

Feet and hands

Parrots are well designed for life in the forests, not just because their color provides camouflage. Their feet are strong and adapted for grasping branches – the two outer toes of the foot point backward and the two inner toes point forward, allowing the birds to clamp onto their perches. Their legs and feet are so strong they can hang from one foot and feed

◀ *The Red-crowned parrot gets its name from the red feathers above its beak.*

using their free foot. The beak also acts like a "third foot" and is used to grapple when climbing through the branches.

Mostly vegetarians, parrots eat a wide range of vegetable matter when feeding in the treetops – fruit, seeds, nectar, and pollen. The stocky bill has a characteristic hook on the top beak that slides over the bottom beak. The beak is delicate enough for preening yet powerful enough to crush hard seeds and nuts. They hold the nuts in place with their tongues and use their lower jaws like chisels to crack the shells of the nuts. Studies of parrot behavior show that larger parrots, with larger bills, can eat much bigger hard-shelled nuts. In this way, several species of parrot can live in a small area because they specialize on different-sized seeds, their primary source of food.

NATURAL HABITAT

Red-crowned parrot

KEY FACTS

- **Name**
Red-crowned parrot or Green-cheeked amazon (*Amazona viridigenalis*)

- **Range**
Northeastern Mexico; escaped cage birds found in southeastern Florida and Los Angeles

- **Habitat**
Woodlands

- **Appearance**
12½ in (32 cm) long; green plumage with a red forehead and wing patch

- **Food**
Fruits, seeds, nuts, buds, and flowers

- **Breeding**
Nest in holes; the female lays two eggs, which she incubates for 28 days; poorly developed young

- **Status**
Endangered due to habitat destruction and capture

Devoted mates

Parrots are devoted to their mates — many species pair for life. To protect their chicks from predators, parrots usually lay their eggs in hollow trees and branches. Sometimes the parrot excavates the hole, but often it "steals" it from another smaller animal. The nest hole is cushioned with any soft plant material the birds can find — such as wood dust, grasses, or leaves. Not all parrots nest in holes. Some species from the plains of Australasia, such as the New Guinean Buff-faced pygmy parrot (*Micropsitta pusio*) and the Golden-shouldered parrot (*Psephotus chrysopterygius*), nest in old termite mounds.

As they fly through the thick forest, parrots use their extremely loud and cackling voices to communicate with one another. They are among the noisiest of birds with a harsh and unmelodic variety of calls. In captivity many species of parrots learn to mimic human voices and this ability to "talk," along with their brilliant plumage, has made them popular cage birds and pets for centuries. No one knows why parrots mimic humans, but the habit indicates that they are relatively intelligent creatures. Many species are very long lived, some have survived in captivity for over 80 years.

Doomed to extinction?

Sadly, many of the larger species (which are thought to be relatively intelligent) become easily bored by captivity and can become destructive. Furthermore, up to 25 percent (approximately 50 species) of all parrots are threatened with extinction or have recently become extinct (about 10 species). In part, this is due to loss of habitat resulting from the destruction of the world's tropical and subtropical forests. However, many species are threatened because too many birds have been collected for the pet trade.

Most species of parrot are sociable and they are usually seen in pairs or flocks. Some of the smaller species (such as the budgerigars) may form enormous flocks. Many species roost together at night, often in very tall or isolated trees so they can keep watch for predators. Predators include tree-living mammals like monkeys, and birds of prey such as hawks and falcons, which rob nests, stealing eggs and young. Most of their enemies seem to be put off by the large flocks and their loud, harsh screams.

▼ The arrangement of a parrot's toes means it can use its feet like hands to grip seeds and other food. Parrots depend so much on their claws that, like people who are left- or right-handed, individuals become left- or right-"footed." This African grey parrot prefers to use its left foot.

See also **Cockatoo, Macaw, Rainforest**

Passionflower

Passionflowers are flowering plants (angiosperms) that belong to the group (genus) *Passiflora*. Most species in this genus are found in tropical Asia, Australia, Central and South America, and Polynesia.

Many of the 400 species of passionflower are herbaceous (they have green, nonwoody stems). All of these plants use modified leaves called tendrils to climb up

▲ *The magnificent, showy flowers of the Scarlet passionflower (Passiflora coccinea) are a common sight in many parts of South America. This plant has become a favorite with gardeners all over the world.*

a neighboring plant. Tendrils are whip-like strands that are extremely sensitive to touch. As they grow out of the stem and encounter an object (such as another plant) close by, the end of the tendril wraps around the object and clings tightly around it. Gradually the tissues inside the tendril strengthen. The entire plant is then supported by this strong anchor point.

Flower shapes

Many passionflowers are highly prized for their showy, unusual flowers. The appearance of passionflower blossoms varies quite widely from species to species. The most common flower forms are either shallow saucer shapes or long, cylindrical or trumpet-shaped tubes. There are five sepals (the sepals enclose the other parts of the flower in bud and open around the base of the petals when the flower blooms), five petals, and many thread-like filaments — all these structures constitute the corona, the most conspicuous part of the flower.

A stalk rises from the center of the flower, with a ring of five stamens (male pollen-producing structures) at the top. Above the stamens is the ovary, which contains the female reproductive cells. On top of the ovary are three widely spreading columns called styles. Each style ends in a button-like structure called a stigma. The pollen sticks to the stigma — an easy target for pollinating insects and birds.

Edible fruits

After pollination and fertilization of the flower, seeds develop inside the fruit. Some passionflowers are important as ornamental plants, especially on the sides of buildings; others are grown commercially for their edible fruits.

NATURAL HABITAT

■ Scarlet passionflower

We eat some of the most highly perfumed passion fruits as delicate dessert fruits. The most notable of these is the Giant granadilla (*Passiflora quadrangularis*). Although the fruit of a passionflower is generally not much larger than a hen's egg, that of the Giant granadilla is enormous: it is like a gourd and may weigh as much as 8 lb (1.8 kg). In addition, the Purple granadilla (*Passiflora edulis*) and the Yellow granadilla or Jamaican honeysuckle (*Passiflora laurifola*) are widely grown in tropical and subtropical countries for their fruit.

Other passionflowers include the Wild passionflower (*Passiflora incarnata*), also known as the Passion vine or the maypop, which climbs to between 10-30 ft (3-9 m) high. It has pink and white flowers about 1½-3 in (4-7.5 cm) across and a berry-like edible fruit about 2 in (5 cm) long. The Scarlet passionflower (*Passiflora coccinea*) is slightly smaller. As its name suggests, this beautiful plant has vivid, scarlet flowers up to 5 in (12.5 cm) across.

KEY FACTS

● **Name**
Scarlet passionflower (*Passiflora coccinea*)

● **Range**
Native to Guianas, southern Venezuela, and the Amazon Basin of Bolivia, Brazil, and Peru; cultivated in many countries as an ornamental plant

● **Habitat**
Tropical rainforests

● **Appearance**
Climbing plant with scarlet flowers up to 5 in (12.5 cm) across; coarse, oval leaves 6 in (15 cm) long

● **Life cycle**
Perennial

● **Uses**
Cultivated for its attractive and unusual flowers

● **Status**
Widely cultivated

Peacock

Since ancient times peacocks have had a close association with humans and have been a graceful sight around many Indian temples and European gardens. They are found in most parts of the world, in parks and gardens where they have been introduced and allowed to roam freely.

Noisy but shy

Peacocks are very large, long-legged, long-necked tropical relatives of the pheasant family. The Common peacock that originally came from India and Sri Lanka is the species of peacocks that most people know. It is remarkable for its breeding display, in which the male fans out his train, displaying his well-known "eyes." The other two species of peacock, from the forests and scrub of India, Southeast Asia, and China, or Zaïre are becoming very rare. Peacocks are shy and furtive

▲ *During the breeding season, the male peacock struts around his display ground with his train fanned out, showing off the wonderful pattern of green, blue, and bronze "eyes." The train contains about 200 feathers and measures about 5 ft (1.5 m) in length, trailing behind the male when it is not fanned out.*

birds, and despite their large size they are very good at hiding in the undergrowth. This is particularly true of the peahens (females) because they have more muted colors than the peacocks (males).

However, these birds have very keen sight and hearing and give loud, raucous shrieks of alarm if intruders encroach on their territory. This is one of the reasons for keeping them in large parks and gardens: they act like guard dogs.

Peacocks feed mainly in the early morning and the late evening. They strut through the undergrowth, pecking at plants and looking for insects. They eat flower buds and seeds, so they are not very popular with gardeners on the estates where they live! However, they do keep the undergrowth free of harmful insects. They also eat snakes and other reptiles or amphibians that they find.

At night peacocks fly up into the branches of trees to roost. They choose perches in high trees so that they can see in all directions. The trees are often out in the open, and several peacocks share the roost. They call loudly as they go up into the trees, and continue their raucous shrieking as they descend in the morning.

Breeding display

It is the behavior of the male at breeding time that gives peacocks their reputation for vanity and pride. Most of the time, the peacocks, with their magnificent peacock blue breasts and heads and greenish-bronze feathers, have long trains

◄ *Peacocks spend most of the year in all-male groups.*

trailing behind them like tails. These trains are special feathers called tail coverts, and their true tails are hidden beneath them.

At the start of the breeding season, the males move away from the rest of the flock that they normally live with. Each cock returns to a place he occupied in previous years and establishes territorial rights. If any other males try to intrude, he uses his claws and the spurs on the back of his feet to fight them.

Within his territory the male has up to four special display sites. He waits near one of these until a group of females approaches and then displays before them. His tail feathers become erect and support the quivering train, spread fan-wise and arched forward over his head. All the time he walks up and down his site with mincing steps. He turns suddenly toward a female, trying to attract her with his magnificent train. The females often appear to run away, but if one hesitates the male catches hold of her and mates with her.

Each male mates with several females during the breeding season. At this time the birds usually form small groups of three or four females and a single male. The females scrape a hollow in the ground for a nest and lay up to six eggs. They tend the eggs without help from the males. The eggs take about four weeks to hatch, and the young are well developed, able to run around a few days after they have emerged from the eggs.

Once the breeding season is over, peacocks tend to form separate groups, with males in one group and females and immature birds in another.

NATURAL HABITAT

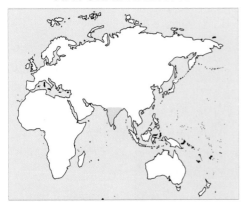

Original range of Common peacock

KEY FACTS

● **Name**
Indian or Common peacock (*Pavo cristatus*)

● **Range**
India and Sri Lanka; in captivity worldwide

● **Habitat**
Forests and scrub

● **Appearance**
Male is 36-48 in (92-122 cm) long (without the train); a shiny, dark-blue head, neck, and breast; a golden-green back, a dull black lower belly; a long train; females are 32-35 in (80-90 cm) long; brown and metallic color with a paler underside

● **Food**
Snakes, flower buds, insects, seeds, lizards

● **Breeding**
Male displays to a group of females, fanning out his train feathers; usually 4-6 eggs laid in a hollow on the ground; the eggs are incubated for about 28 days

● **Status**
Common

See also **Pheasant**

Peccary

Peccaries look almost like pigs on stilts. Like pigs, they have very large heads, upright ears, long flattened snouts, bristly coats, and small tails. However, their legs are longer and more slender than pigs' and end in small, dainty hoofs.

Safety in numbers

Like wild pigs, peccaries have long teeth in their jaws. These are canines, or "dog teeth," which are on both the top and the bottom jaw and are so large they look like small tusks. These teeth are not only long, they are almost like pointed daggers, with the upper ones rubbing against the lower ones to keep them sharp. As well as being useful for rooting around in the dirt for food (mostly plant roots and tubers), these tusks are also very important for defense from predators, which include jaguars,

pumas, bobcats, and coyotes. There is also safety in numbers, and group defense is the peccaries' main strategy against predators. When in danger, the young are sheltered between the rear legs of the adults in the group.

Collared peccaries live in herds of 5 to 15, with some groups containing up to 50 animals. In Peru, where Collared peccaries have been studied in the rainforests, herds of these creatures can be found by listening for them as they crunch away on fallen nuts and fruit. Herds are territorial, with their territories usually surrounding an essential water hole and wallow. The

▼ *This mother and her babies are foraging. They have a good sense of smell and can detect roots up to 3 in (8 cm) underground. They dig them out with their large snouts and tusk-like teeth.*

KEY FACTS

● **Name**
Collared peccary
(*Tayassu tajacu*)

● **Range**
From Arizona and Texas down to northern Argentina

● **Habitat**
Scrub, rainforests

● **Appearance**
A large pig-like animal, measuring 37 in (94 cm) with a short tail; a dark gray-brown, bristly coat, with a white collar around the neck in adults; the young are reddish with a dark stripe down their backs

● **Feeding**
Mainly vegetarian: succulent roots, tubers, cactus fruit, palm nuts; may also eat some grubs and snakes, or other small vertebrates

● **Breeding**
1-4 well-developed young are suckled for 6-8 weeks and stay with their mother until they are about 2-3 months old

● **Status**
Widespread

herd is subdivided into small family groups and these may separate to search for food when it is scarce.

Marking the territory

Peccary herds mark their territory in two ways. Firstly they concentrate their dung in piles, marking the boundaries of their range. These dung heaps are also important to the forest ecology, because they contain many undigested seeds that often begin to grow in the dung piles. Secondly, peccaries mark their territories by rubbing scent from their rumps against tree trunks. This scent also allows members of the group to recognize each other. This is important because peccaries have very poor eyesight and use smell to tell the difference between friends and enemies, as well as to detect food.

Collared peccaries are efficient breeders, and they are able to breed throughout the year. Just before they give birth, females leave the herd and hide in a thicket, hollow log, cave, or burrow. The young are well developed and can run within a

▲ *Of the three species of peccary, the Collared peccary (Tayassu tajacu), shown above, is the most common. It is found from Texas all the way south to Argentina.*

few hours of being born. This allows the mother and her piglets to rejoin the herd only a day after the birth. Rearing of the young, like much of peccary life, is a group affair. Frequently, the mother is assisted in nursing and caring for her young by a "nursemaid" (often an older sister). In this way the young will survive even if the mother dies.

While the Collared peccary is very common, the other two species of peccary are extremely rare. The White-lipped peccary (*Tayassu pecari*) is darker and larger, and has white lips instead of the white collar of the Collared peccary. It occurs from southern Mexico to northeastern Argentina, but is always rare. The Chacoan peccary (*Catagonus wagneri*), found only in Paraguay, Argentina, and Bolivia, is so rare that it was only "discovered" by scientists in the 1970s.

NATURAL HABITAT

☐ Collared peccary

Pelican

The pelican is a strange-looking bird, with a large body, short legs, and a huge bill. Its proportions are quite different from those of most other birds. Its most remarkable feature is the huge pouch that hangs from the lower part of its long bill. This is used as a fishing net when the pelican goes in search of food.

Shapes and sizes

Pelicans are among the largest living birds, growing up to 6 ft (2 m) long. There are seven species found in different parts of the world, mainly in tropical and subtropical areas near the sea. The pelicans of the world are divided into three groups: the mainly white species, the large tree-nesting species, and the brown species. The white pelican of North America lives in cooler zones, on inland waterways and lakes rather than coastal regions. The other species found in North America is the Brown pelican. It lives on the Florida and Gulf coasts, in southern California, and through Central and South America.

Pelicans are long-lived birds: one specimen in a zoo was recorded to have lived for 54 years. In the wild, the average lifespan is about 20 years.

Dipping and diving

Different species of pelican have various methods of fishing. The American white pelican may fish on its own or in groups.

▼ *The Brown pelican is a seabird rarely found on inland waterways. Like other brown and gray species, the Brown pelican nests in large colonies.*

KEY FACTS

- **Name**
American white pelican (*Pelecanus erythrorhynchos*)

- **Range**
Southern Canada to the southern U.S., winters in Costa Rica

- **Habitat**
Inland lakes

- **Appearance**
50-70 in (125-75 cm) long, wingspan of 8-9$\frac{1}{2}$ ft (240-285 cm); a very large white bird with black wing tips and an orange-salmon bill; the legs are orange-red

- **Food**
Mainly fish, occasionally salamanders and crayfish

- **Breeding**
Islands in brackish and freshwater lakes, in colonies of up to several hundred; 1-6 eggs, usually 2; male and female incubate the eggs for about 36 days; the young are fed on predigested fish; they first fly at about 60 days

- **Status**
Common

If it is alone, it flies over its hunting ground. On a calm day it usually flies at quite a height — over 50 ft (15 m) from the surface of the water. If it is flying into the wind, it usually skims the surface of the water; at this low level there is less wind resistance, and it gets some lift from the wind bouncing off the surface.

When the pelican spots its prey it dives toward the water. It breaks the surface with the soles of its feet and dips its large bill just under the water to catch the fish. Sometimes, groups of American white pelicans fish together. They swim together in a group, searching for likely prey. When they spot the fish they drive them into shallower water where it is easier to catch them.

The Brown pelican has a slightly different method of fishing. Again, it starts by flying over the sea, and when it spots its prey it dives right under the surface of the water to catch it. It may dive from as high as 60 or 70 ft (18 or 20 m), entering the water with a great splash.

Like all species, the Brown pelican has special air sacs under its skin, and its bones hold pockets of air. The air sacs cushion the impact as it hits the water, and then all the air in its body means that it bounces back up to the surface like a cork. As it surfaces it is always facing into the wind, ready to take off again.

However the pelicans manage to catch their prey, they sieve it in the same way. The lower part of the bill may hold up to 3 gal (15 litres) of water and fish. The pelican squeezes out the water by contracting the skin that forms the lower part of its bill, allowing the water to flow

out of the corners of its mouth. Then it swallows the fish that are left. It never carries food (or water) around in its beak. Pelicans have large wingspans, and once airborne they fly very gracefully.

Messy nests

Pelicans are a bit lazy when it comes to nesting; in many cases the pairs build no nest at all, but sometimes they scrape together a mound of dirt and debris on which to lay their eggs. The female incubates the eggs for over a month. Both parents work to feed the newly hatched young. They appear to feed from their parents' beaks, but in fact they are putting their heads right into the adults' throats to feed on partly digested fish.

▲ *In order to support such a large body, the pelican is an expert fisherman. It has to eat about 4 lb (2 kg) of fish per day to keep going. This American white is landing on the water to make a catch. Pelicans have webbed feet that they use when swimming.*

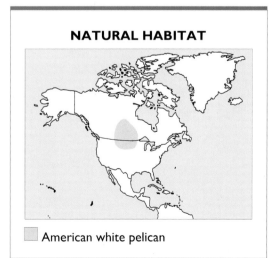

NATURAL HABITAT

American white pelican

Penguin

Penguins are flightless, sea-loving birds of the cooler parts of the southern hemisphere. Most are found south of the line of latitude at 45 degrees south — in southern South America, Antarctica, and the islands around Antarctica. Some penguins are found further north (in South Africa, Australia, New Zealand, and even on the Galapagos Islands near the equator). In these places, there are currents of cold water flowing north from the polar seas.

Snappy dressers

Penguins are well suited to their marine lifestyle, equally at home swimming horizontally through the water or standing upright on land. They are often described as smartly dressed birds, with white bibs and black backs and flippers. These feathers are vital: they provide the birds with the insulation they need both in the water and on their cold, polar breeding grounds. The feathers are in three short and dense layers, growing thickly all over the body, and they act as a waterproof

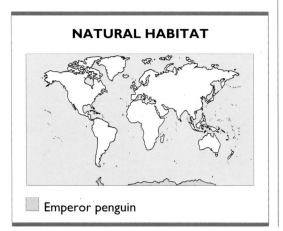

NATURAL HABITAT

[ ] Emperor penguin

coat. The shiny surface of the wet feathers helps the birds to glide through the water.

When they swim their bodies are highly streamlined. They stretch their beaks out in front of them and use their wings as flippers to propel themselves through the water; their webbed feet and tails act as rudders to steer them. They can bend and turn with amazing speed as they chase their food under the water.

Penguins have short, stout bills with a strong grip to hold onto their prey. The marine creatures that they chase include crustaceans, fish, and squid.

Father figures

All species of penguin come ashore to breed. They form large colonies, huddling together against the cold in the southern part of their range. Males usually pair up with the same females year after year.

▲ *Penguins feed their young by regurgitating fish so that the chicks can take the food from their mouths. This is a Gentoo penguin from Elephant Island in Antarctica.*

▶ *The male Emperor penguins care for the eggs and feed the young. After the eggs have hatched, the young birds flock together in groups called crèches. Adult birds take turns to tend the young and catch fish for food.*

Perhaps the most remarkable breeding habits are those of the Emperor penguin. Emperor penguins endure extremely cold conditions during their breeding season. The average temperature is -4°F (-20°C), with an added wind chill factor that makes it feel even colder. Breeding penguins get very hungry: because they choose to breed a long way from the open sea, they cannot eat while they are tending the eggs or the young.

It is the male Emperor penguins that do most of the work. After the females have laid their eggs, the males gather in large groups of up to 5000 birds. They huddle together for warmth with as many as 10 birds per sq yd (11 birds per m²) with their eggs on their feet. A pouch-like fold of skin hangs down from the body, and this keeps the egg warm. Due to the winds, the males on one side of the group get colder than those in the center. So the exposed birds move around, with their eggs balanced on their feet, to the more sheltered side of the group. Each bird has to endure some of the cold, and each gets a turn in the center of the group. They become very cooperative, and suppress nearly all their aggressive behavior.

In many other species of penguin, the parents share the work of tending the eggs so that each gets a chance to feed.

Vulnerability

The young penguins used to be fairly secure in the cold Antarctic wastelands because there were no mammals to attack them. Skuas and other predatory birds may attack from time to time, and the adult birds are also chased by marine predators such as Killer whales, seals (especially Leopard seals), and sharks. However, the introduction of mammals and the arrival of humans have meant that some species are now listed as threatened. Oil pollution and competition with commercial fishing boats for their food have also put many species at risk.

KEY FACTS

- **Name**
  Emperor penguin
  (*Aptenodytes forsteri*)

- **Range**
  Antarctic continent and seas to the edge of the ice pack

- **Appearance**
  Largest penguin, 40-50 in (100-130 cm) high; the upperparts are blue-gray, the underparts are white; a small, black head with large yellow-white patches on the sides of the head; a slender, curved bill, which is black with an orange, pink, or lilac stripe

- **Breeding**
  Breeding colonies form in the fall; the female lays a single egg; the male incubates the egg on his feet for 60 days; both parents undertake a long fast during courtship, incubation, and brooding, lasting for up to 120 days for the male and 64 days for the female; both parents feed the chicks from late winter to spring so that the young are independent by the summer

- **Status**
  Common

See also **Ocean, Polar regions, Seal, Whale**

Perch

The perch is a freshwater fish that is popular among sportsmen and is commercially fished in many areas. Perch are found in lakes and slow-moving rivers all around the northern hemisphere. In North America the proper name of the perch is the Yellow perch (*Perca flavescens*); in northwestern Europe and Eurasia there is an almost identical species called the European perch (*Perca fluviatilis*). These two species are so similar that some scientists think that one is a subspecies of the other.

Weedy hideouts

Perch are typical fish of lowland rivers and lakes, often swimming in small schools, although large perch tend to be solitary. They are still for most of the day, gently moving their fins and tail so that they do not drift with the current. They lurk in the weeds or between tree roots, and they are often found near wharfs and jetties. Their neutral colors help to disguise them

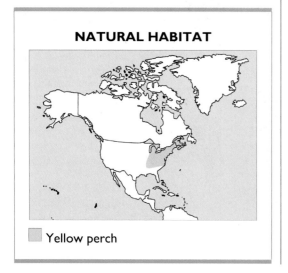

NATURAL HABITAT

☐ Yellow perch

in the murky water. The color may vary according to the place where the fish live: in areas where there is a lot of weed and algae, for example, they are likely to be green, but those that live in muddy or sandy habitats are more likely to be brown or yellow. Although they like slow-moving water, they are rarely found in stagnant or brackish water.

Adult perch have to contend with the keen fishermen who hunt them for sport or for food. If they survive, they may live for as long as nine or ten years. By this time they may weigh as much as 10 lb (4.5 kg), but most do not reach more than 5 lb (2.3 kg).

Breeding

The perch of the northern hemisphere lay eggs in the reeds and weeds along the edges of the rivers and lakes where they live. At the start of the spawning season in the spring, the colors of the males become more intense: they may be any color from

▲ *The Yellow perch is a deep-bodied fish with yellow, blue-green, or brown coloring. It has distinctive dark bars across its back.*

▶ *When the female perch spawns (breeds) she releases a long string of eggs encased in jelly. This sticks to plants or to the bed of the river, and the male perch then releases milt (sperm) to fertilize the eggs. The eggs remain in the jelly, which helps to protect them until the young perch hatch.*

bronze-green to bright yellow, with dark bars forming a pattern down their backs. Their lower fins turn an orange-red color.

The adults move upstream into shallow waters to spawn. The female may lay more than 100,000 eggs at night or early in the morning. The total number of eggs she lays increases with the size of the female. The eggs themselves are transparent and are held in a string of transparent jelly that is folded in neat, concertina-like pleats.

The strings of eggs may be as long as 7 ft (2.1 m) and as wide as 2-4 in (5-10 cm). They stick to plants or to the bottom of the riverbed, where they are fertilized by the male. After the eggs have been laid, the adults return to their deeper water habitats. The eggs hatch in about eight to ten days. The young are transparent when they first hatch, turning silver or pale green. They live in large schools to increase the chances of survival.

The young perch grow rapidly, feeding on tiny insect larvae and other young fish. They are fully grown and ready to breed in three or four years.

African cousins

Because they were such popular fish in Europe, perch have been introduced to most parts of the world where Europeans have settled, including Australia and South Africa. The Yellow and European perches were not originally found in Africa; however, there are several species that have been given the name perch because they were similar to European perch, including the Nile perch. This fish is found throughout the Nile system, and in the river basins of eastern Africa, the Volta, the Niger, the Zaïre, and Lake Chad.

See also **Lake, river, and estuary**

Petrel

◄ *Although most petrels are small birds, this Southern giant petrel is almost as large as an albatross.*

KEY FACTS

● **Name**
Wilson's storm petrel *(Oceanites oceanicus)*

● **Range**
Worldwide apart from North Pacific

● **Habitat**
Open seas and coasts

● **Appearance**
7 in (17.5 cm) long; a wingspan of 15-16½ in (38-42 cm); sooty brown or black, a white rump patch; a black bill; a short, square tail

● **Food**
Plankton, small fish, squid; waste from ships

● **Breeding**
Female lays 1 white egg from Dec-Jan; the eggs are incubated for 39-48 days; the young are fed by both parents

● **Status**
Common

The name "petrel" covers a great number of seabirds, spread over several different bird families. Of the many species, the storm petrels are the most intriguing. There are about 20 different species within this family. The most common of these is Wilson's storm petrel; indeed, some scientists think that there are more of this particular species than of any other species of bird in the world. However, two species, Markham's storm petrel and the Ringed storm petrel are threatened.

Storm petrels spend all their time at sea, apart from when they are breeding. They are seen over most of the world's oceans, particularly in the southern hemisphere.

Delicate looks

Storm petrels are small birds compared to most other seabirds, only 5-10 in (13-25 cm) in length. They are sprightly in flight, and are most often seen following ships sailing the southern oceans. They have a relatively short, hooked beak, with tubular nostrils fused to the top of it. (This is a distinctive feature of several families of seabirds.) They are dark-colored birds, with a band of white feathers across their tails. They have slender legs that do not weigh them down as they fly, and they have webbed feet to help them swim if they land on the water. Although they roam over the world's most distant oceans, they are not solitary birds. They usually gather in small groups or pairs, and in the breeding season they gather together in large colonies.

When they are in the air, they are constantly on the lookout for food. They have a very controlled flight, and sometimes they look as though they are walking on the water: they flap their wings and "paddle" the water with their feet, hovering just above the surface, so that they can easily snatch their meals from beneath without having to get their feathers wet. It is this habit that gives them their name. "Petrel" is derived from Peter, after St. Peter, who according to the Bible actually walked on water.

Since they spend so much time in the air, these birds are not very good at walking on land. They often flap their wings to help themselves along in the same way as they do at sea.

Moving south

When the summer comes to the cold regions in and around Antarctica, Wilson's storm petrel and many of its relatives arrive, too. Great colonies of the various species, often numbering many thousands of birds, flock together to mate and nest. By day, however, you might not even know the birds were there. During the breeding season, the birds are only active at night, and they build their nests in burrows or rock crevices so they are safe from predators. Pairs return to the same nesting burrow year after year, remaining faithful to each other for life. Both male and female work to dig the burrow in the first year (or repair it in subsequent years). There is a short courtship display (at night) and then the female lays a single egg. The incubation period is quite long – 5½-7 weeks. Once the egg has hatched, both parents work to feed the young, bringing the oily food that they have eaten back into their mouths so that the young can digest it easily.

Although they tend the young chick until it has its true flight feathers, storm petrels apparently believe in throwing their young in at the deep end. Once they are ready to fly, the parents desert the burrow and the young finds its way out and takes its maiden flight alone.

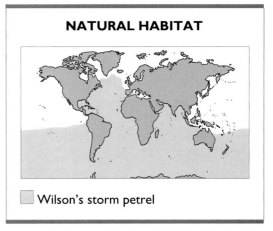

NATURAL HABITAT

☐ Wilson's storm petrel

▼ *A Wilson's storm petrel soars over its icy breeding grounds, seaching for food. Its food includes shrimp and other crustaceans, mollusks, squid, and all the small organisms that make up the plankton that drifts in the ocean. It also feeds on oil and blubber from wounded whales or seals.*

See also **Ocean, Polar regions, Tide pool and coast**

Pheasant

Pheasants originally came from Asia, where there are over 20 different species. They are mainly ground-dwelling forest birds, and they are found in tropical rainforests and more temperate forests in the mountains of central Asia. However, many species are popular game birds among hunters, and they have been introduced in most parts of the world.

Widely spread

In North America, Ring-necked pheasants are found across Canada and the northern part of the United States. Rather than the enclosed forest habitats of Asia, they are found in woodlands and farmlands, where they use hedges for cover. Hedges also act as "travel lanes" enabling them to move around their territory almost invisibly.

The first pheasants to be brought to North America were introduced as game birds in Oregon in the 1880s; they must have liked their new home because ten

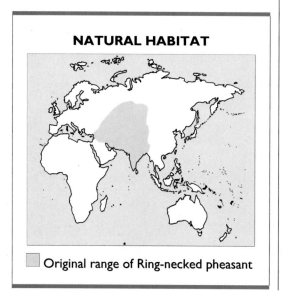

NATURAL HABITAT

Original range of Ring-necked pheasant

years later 50,000 birds were reported to have been shot in a single day. Since then they have become one of the most widely distributed and popular game birds. As well as being popular for sport and as food, many species are very ornamental. The Golden pheasant (*Chrysolophus pictus*) from the mountains of China, and Lady Amherst's pheasant (*C. amherstiae*) from the mountains of southeast Tibet and southwest China to northern Burma, are sometimes kept as pets.

Scraping a living

Pheasants are large, chicken-like birds with long, pointed tails. They have long, strong legs with clawed feet, which, together with their bills, they use to scratch the

▲ *Male pheasants often fight with each other for a particular female or group of females. Although the birds have sharp claws and beaks, the fights rarely result in injury.*

▶ *The male Ring-necked pheasant is a fine bird often seen on farmlands. The average lifespan for males is 10 months and for females 20 months.*

ground for food. They are not very choosey about their food, pecking at seeds, buds, and other plant matter and sometimes eating insects.

Pheasants live in areas with plenty of vegetation, so they do not need to travel far. They rarely move more than a couple of miles away from their nesting sites. As they strut around their homes, pheasants are well camouflaged. However, if disturbed they can be heard taking flight with a noisy whirring sound. Although this is meant to deter predators, it makes them an easy target for hunters.

Courting rituals

The males, with their often spectacular plumage, perform long and elaborate rituals to attract mates. The male Ring-necked pheasant struts around in front of the females with the crests (ear tufts) on the side of his head raised. He has a bare patch of skin around his eyes that turns red and swells to attract a female.

Each male usually mates with a group of two to four females. Each female builds a nest in the male's territory – usually just a hollow in the ground lined with grasses and hidden by vegetation. The male patrols the territory and fights off any males that try to intrude. The females take care of the eggs, and in most species the chicks are already well developed when they hatch.

The female continues to protect her chicks because they are very vulnerable; she uses the "wounded bird" act (she pretends that she is injured and therefore attractive game) to lure away predators. In the fall, the end of the breeding season, many families form flocks of up to 30 or 40 birds and occasionally up to 400.

Short life

Perhaps because of human hunters, but also because of their vulnerablility, the Ring-necked pheasant has a short lifespan. Many of the young that hatch in the spring do not live beyond October. More than a third of the total species of pheasant are endangered in the wild; fortunately many species have been bred in captivity.

KEY FACTS

● **Name**
Ring-necked or Common pheasant (*Phasianus colchicus*)

● **Range**
Originally from Asia, now worldwide

● **Habitat**
Mainly cultivated farmland with hedges

● **Appearance**
Male: 30-36 in (75-95 cm) long including tail of 21 in (52 cm); rich bronze with brown, black, and white markings on back; head and neck a shiny green-blue; white collar; patch of bright red skin on cheeks and around eyes; female: mottled brown, 21-25 in (52-62 cm) including tail of 11-12 in (27-30 cm)

● **Food**
Waste grain, seeds, also nuts, fruits, and some insects

● **Breeding**
Male mates with 2-4 hens; 5-23 (usually 10-12) eggs; the eggs take 23-25 days to hatch; the young can feed themselves, but their parents help them to find food

● **Status**
Widespread

Pine

Pines are evergreen trees or conifers. They belong to the group (genus) *Pinus*, which is made up of about 90 species of cone-bearing plants. Pines are valuable trees. They are used to make many important products, including paper and timber.

Pines are most common in the moderately cold (temperate) regions of the northern hemisphere. However, some species are distributed much farther south. Many pines thrive in parts of tropical and subtropical Indonesia, Nicaragua, and North Africa.

Shapes and sizes

Pine trees have grooved bark, oily wood, and straight trunks. Branches emerge from the top of the trunk in distinctive swirling

▲ *The Scots pine (Pinus sylvestris) is a common tree found throughout most of Europe and western and northern Asia. It is an extremely hardy pine. It thrives in almost any climate and in dry, nutrient-poor soil. This makes the Scots pine a popular choice for reforestation.*

shapes. The needle-like leaves of pines grow in bunches of one, two, three, or five. A protective case holds the bunches of needles to the stem at their base. The needles remain on the tree for between two to 12 years.

Pine cones are the reproductive structures of the tree. The cones mature at the end of their second year. Then they either drop from the tree or remain attached, shedding their winged seeds on dry, windy days at the end of the winter.

The largest known pine is the Sugar pine (*Pinus lambertiana*), found in Oregon and California in the United States. This species is about 200-245 ft (60-70 m) tall, with a trunk up to 12 ft (3.5 m) across.

Hard and soft pines

Botanists divide pines into two main groups: hard and soft. As their name

NATURAL HABITAT

■ Scots pine

● **Name**

Scots pine
(*Pinus sylvestris*)

● **Range**

Widely distributed in
Europe and northern
and western Asia

● **Habitat**

Dense forests

● **Appearance**

Tall tree, reaching
up to 130 ft (40 m);
straight trunk topped
with a crown of
paired, bluish-green
needles; red female
flowers up to ⅖ in
(1 cm) across; male
flowers yellow; cones
3 in (8 cm) across,
bearing winged seeds

● **Life cycle**

Perennial

● **Uses**

Reforestation; timber;
tar and turpentine

● **Status**

Widespread

▶ *The female cones of the Scots pine become brown and woody with age. Like other conifers, the Scots pine bears both male and female cones. These structures contain the tree's reproductive cells.*

suggests, hard pines produce mostly hard, strong wood. Their needles commonly form in bunches of two or three.

One of the most famous hard pines is the Scots pine (*Pinus sylvestris*), which is found throughout Europe and northern and western Asia. This tree grows to heights of 70-130 ft (20-40 m) and has a mushroom-shaped crown of foliage on top of a straight trunk about 3 ft (1 m) across. It has reddish-brown bark, and its twisted branches are thickly covered with bluish-green needles.

By contrast, soft pines produce mainly soft wood. Soft pines usually have bunches of five needles, although some have bunches of one to four needles. The Western white pine (*Pinus monticola*) is a soft pine. It can grow at altitudes of up to 10,000 ft (3000 m) and is found from southern British Columbia in Canada to the mountains of the Sierra Nevada in California.

A useful group of trees

Pine trees are cultivated for their wood, which is used for timber and to produce

pulp to make paper. The most important pines used in the U.S. timber industry are the Long-leaf pine (*Pinus palustris*), the Loblolly pine (*Pinus taeda*), and the Caribbean pitch pine (*Pinus caribaea*). The Long-leaf pine is also a major source of oils, resin, tar, and turpentine. The secondary by-products of pine distillation include charcoal and lampblack (a finely powdered black soot used as a pigment). Many pines are so rich in oil and resin that they easily ignite. As a result, forest fires are a real threat to their survival.

Pines are widely grown as ornamentals – the Austrian pine (*Pinus nigra*) and the Himalayan pine (*Pinus griffithii*) are the most popular species. Pines grow especially well on land that is open, windswept, and well drained. They may even flourish in nutrient-poor soil, which makes them a favorite choice for reforestation. In addition, most mature pines can tolerate drought. However, they do need full sunlight and clean air for healthy growth and reproduction.

Hardy pine species have many other uses, too. The Black pine (*Pinus thunbergii*), native to Japan, is used to reclaim sand dunes. Another species, the Maritime pine or pinaster (*Pinus pinaster*), is used to stabilize dune drifts on the coasts of the Mediterranean and the Bay of Biscay off the coast of western Europe.

See also **Larch, Sequoia, Temperate forest**

Pine marten

An acrobat of the trees, the long, sleek pine marten chases birds and small mammals such as squirrels through the treetops with incredible speed and nimbleness. It is closely related to other martens such as the fisher and the sable, and it belongs to the same family as weasels, polecats, mink, ferrets, badgers,

NATURAL HABITAT

☐ American pine marten

▲ *Many scientists believe that the four species of pine marten found throughout Eurasia and North America are, in fact, the same species, differing only slightly in size and in the extent of the white bib, or throat patch. The European pine marten is the largest subspecies, and the American pine marten is the smallest.*

skunks, and otters. Like all martens, the pine marten is specially adapted to preying on animals that live in trees, and is able to catch all but the fastest prey.

Despite its skill in running through the trees, the pine marten spends much of its time on the ground. Here, it hunts for partridges, rabbits, and chipmunks. The pine marten must be careful, however, because a predator can also become the prey, and large birds may try to catch the pine marten if they can. The male pine marten is larger than the female. This difference in size between males and females is thought to reduce competition for food between the two sexes, because the smaller females target much smaller prey than the larger males.

Hanging on until the end

Like the small cats, members of the weasel family (the *Mustelids*) kill small prey by delivering a precise bite to the neck, severing the spinal cord. Martens will sometimes use the same tactics on slightly larger prey such as rabbits, despite the fact that this does not always actually kill them. However, while the small cats rely on a quick, clean kill, the smaller weasels have developed large neck muscles to maintain their grip on struggling victims that may take some time to die of exhaustion, loss of blood, or fright.

The pine marten is a fairly solitary animal, spending most of its time alone on its own territory. It is mainly nocturnal (active at night), perhaps to avoid other predators, but also because it may be easier to catch prey that is unaware at night. During the day, the marten hides away in hollows in trees, such as those used by squirrels, or in woodpecker holes. In the winter it does not hibernate, but may move to lower altitudes to hunt.

Waiting until the time is right

Although the pine marten mates in the summer, its young are not born until the following spring. This would suggest a gestation period (the time a baby takes to grow inside its mother) of eight or nine months – an extremely long time for such a small animal. In fact, the gestation time is much shorter, perhaps 28 days. The confusion arises because the pine marten has what is known as delayed implantation: the fertilized eggs do not start to develop right away, but stay inactive inside the female for several months before they begin to grow. This

allows each pine marten to move away and live a solitary life in the winter when food is scarce, without worrying about finding a mate at exactly the right time.

The European pine marten is slightly larger than the American pine marten, although the two are otherwise very similar in appearance and habits. The pine marten was almost hunted to extinction in North America, where its fur was known as "American sable." By the early twentieth century, numbers had fallen severely, particularly in the northern parts of its range (Alaska, Canada, and the northern United States) due to trapping. They were then declared protected, and there were attempts to reintroduce the pine marten into some states where it had become extinct. Numbers are now increasing.

▼ *Like other martens, pine martens are expert at climbing trees and can leap nimbly from branch to branch in pursuit of their prey.*

KEY FACTS

● **Name**
American pine marten
(*Martes americana*)

● **Range**
From Alaska and Canada down to California and across to New York and New England

● **Habitat**
Coniferous forests

● **Appearance**
Long, slender body 12.6-17.7 in (32-45 cm); males are larger than females; a thick, glossy, browr. coat with pale brown underparts; the legs and long, bushy tail are dark, almost black; the head is pale gray

● **Food**
Fruit, small mammals, birds, insects, and carrion (dead meat)

● **Breeding**
Males and females mate in the summer, but the 1-5 blind and helpless young are not born until the following spring; they open their eyes after 39 days, are weaned in about 6 weeks, and reach adult size after $3\frac{1}{2}$ months

● **Status**
Widespread

See also **Weasel**

Pipefish

◀ *The Great pipefish has mottled coloring that blends with the rocky seabed.*

KEY FACTS

● **Name**
Great pipefish
(*Syngnathus acus*)

● **Range**
European coast of
North Atlantic and
Mediterranean Sea

● **Habitat**
Around the coast
on sandy or muddy
seabed

● **Appearance**
12 in (30 cm) long;
eel-shaped with a
long, tube-like snout;
large tail fin; brown
and beige coloring

● **Food**
Larval and small
fishes, plankton

● **Breeding**
Female passes eggs
to male, who
fertilizes them and
incubates them
between folds of skin
on his belly; the
young can swim away
when they hatch

● **Status**
Common

Pipefish are extraordinary looking fish that are found in the shallow part of seas and oceans worldwide. As their name suggests they are long, thin, eel-like fish. They often swim or rest in a vertical position, so that their bodies are disguised among strands of seaweed where they live.

NATURAL HABITAT

☐ Great pipefish

Shapes and sizes

There are over 300 different species of pipefish. More than a dozen species are found along the Atlantic and Pacific coasts of North America. Two species live in the open Atlantic ocean rather than shallow coastal waters, floating in the masses of sargassum seaweed that are sometimes found there. A few species have adapted to freshwater habitats, and are found in lakes, streams, and rivers, particularly in southern Asia.

One of the larger species is the Great pipefish (*Syngnathus acus*), which is found in the waters around Europe, from Norway to Portugal, and through the

Mediterranean. Rather than floating in seaweed, this pipefish disguises itself by burrowing in the sand on the seabed. The largest pipefish is thought to be the Kelp pipefish (*Syngnathus californiensis*), which grows up to 18 in (45 cm) long. The smallest known species is the Blue-striped pipefish, which is no more than $2^1/_2$ in (6 cm) long. It is widely distributed around the Indo-Pacific coastlines.

Defensive action

Pipefish have stiff bodies that are covered with rows of plates (like some lizards are) rather than the scales normally found on fish. This means that they have difficulty moving to escape predators, so they rely on their shape and color for camouflage. Because they do not swim, they have poorly developed fins – a pair of small pectoral fins on either side of their heads and a flattened dorsal (back) fin at the point where the body tapers into the tail.

The mouth of a pipefish is a round opening at the end of its long snout, and it uses it to suck up its prey – the larval fish, young and small crustaceans, and algae that grow around the seaweed where the pipefish lives.

Father care

The most remarkable feature of the pipefish family is their breeding habits. Like other fish, the female produces large numbers of eggs in the breeding season. The pair perform a mating ritual, intertwining their bodies. The eggs emerge from the female and stick to the belly of the male. In some species there is a special groove on his belly for extra protection.

The male fertilizes the eggs, and they remain stuck to his body until they hatch several weeks later. Because the incubation period is long, the young are well developed when they hatch and are strong enough to swim away from their father.

▼ *The Sargassum pipefish is extremely well disguised as it swims within the sargassum seaweed of the open ocean.*

See also **Kelp and other seaweeds, Ocean, Sea horse**

Piranha

Piranhas have the reputation of being savage maneaters. Indeed, you might imagine they were huge fish, like sharks. The largest of the piranhas, however, is only just over 2 ft (60 cm) long. It is the size of the groups of piranhas that makes them such a threat.

Tropical hunters

Piranhas are found in the rivers flowing through the Amazon basin in South America. There are about 12 known species, divided into three different genera (groups). The largest piranha is called *Pygocentrus piraya*; the best known species is probably the White or Spotted piranha (*Serrasalmus rhombeus*); and the species that is most widespread, with the worst

▲ *The jaws of piranhas do not look very threatening, but they conceal sharp triangular teeth that lock firmly together when the fish bite. Local tribespeople take the jaws of dead piranhas and use the teeth as tools and weapons. They may also try to catch piranhas for their tasty flesh. However, they are tricky to catch and have to be handled with care.*

reputation, is Natterer's or Red piranha (*Rooseveltiella nattereri*). It is this last species that is reported as having attacked humans. White piranhas have been kept in aquariums, but they need a lot of space or they are likely to attack other fish.

Piranhas play an important role as scavengers in the tropical rivers of South America. Their diet consists mainly of injured or dying fish, reptiles, amphibians, and mammals. They are voracious feeders. If an animal falls in the river, they can pick it clean within minutes – even if it is the size of a small pig. The piranhas take clean bites of the flesh using their sharp, strong, triangular teeth. They nibble about a cubic inch (16 cm^3) at a time, stripping their victim down to its skeleton. During

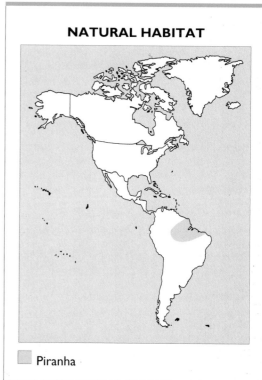

NATURAL HABITAT

Piranha

the frenzy, the piranhas often snap at each other, and many of their number may become victims themselves. However, tales of people being savaged are a little exaggerated. Piranhas are only likely to go for humans if they are bleeding profusely.

Built for the kill

Piranhas have short, stocky bodies that are deeper from back to belly than most river fish. They have a blunt nose and short, powerful jaws. Their teeth are triangular and razor sharp, locking together so the fish can take a clean bite. Piranhas have toothed edges on many of their scales, which make them difficult to grasp, and they are reputed to go on biting even when they are dead.

Although they do attack creatures as large as ponies or alligators, most of the time piranhas feed on small fish, particularly those that are weak or dying. They also eat carrion, helping to keep the river clean. Some species are vegetarian.

Exotic relatives

Piranhas are closely related to some of the most colorful freshwater fish, the tetras, which are popular aquarium specimens.

The Neon tetra (*Paracheirodon innesi*) gets its name from the luminous green and red stripes down its sides. The Splashing tetra lays its eggs on the underside of a leaf, out of reach of predators. The mating pair leap clear of the water, deposit and fertilize their eggs, and then fall back into the water. During the few days it takes for the eggs to hatch, the male Splashing tetra, true to his name, splashes the eggs several times an hour to keep them moist. When the eggs hatch the young drop into the water and swim off.

KEY FACTS

● **Name**
Pygocentrus piraya

● **Range**
Widely distributed in the lower Amazon Basin

● **Habitat**
Fresh water

● **Appearance**
Body up to 14 in (35 cm) long; a deep-bodied fish; belly edged with sharp-toothed scales; a blunt head with short powerful jaws and triangular, razor-sharp teeth

● **Food**
Carnivorous, feeding on mammals, reptiles, and fish including other piranhas

● **Breeding**
Eggs are shed by the female and fertilized by the male; the young have no parental care

● **Status**
Common

◀ *The larger the school of piranhas, the faster any unlucky victims are devoured. If there is blood in the water, the fish become even more frenzied.*

Pitcher plant

Pitcher plants are carnivorous plants that depend on small animal prey for their food. This is because the soil they live in is poor in nutrients. As their name suggests, they produce large, vase- or trumpet-like pitchers. These form as the long leaves of the plants curl upward and join together. They are often topped by a "hood" or "lid."

The name "pitcher plant" is given to a wide range of species, encompassing a huge variety of pitcher shapes and sizes. The Purple or Common pitcher plant (*Sarracenia purpurea*) is the most abundant in North America, living in lakes, ponds, streams, and marshy environments.

▲ *The California pitcher plant's greenish-yellow pitchers are formed from its long leaves. The pitchers have a hood and "fangs," which resemble a cobra's fangs. This gives the plant its other common name – the Cobra lily.*

There are three separate families of pitcher plant: the *Sarraceniaceae,* the *Nepenthaceae,* and the *Cephalotaceae.*

The *Sarraceniaceae* includes several common pitcher plants (*Sarracenia* spp.) from eastern North America, the California pitcher plant (*Darlingtonia californica*), and a few sun pitchers (*Heliamphora* spp.), which are found only on particular plateaux in southeastern Venezuela and Guyana.

The second family, *Nepenthaceae,* is made up of around 70 tropical species (*Nepenthes* spp.), some of which are climbers from the rainforests of Australia, India, Madagascar, and Southeast Asia.

The third family, *Cephalotaceae,* contains just one species, the Albany pitcher plant or Flycatcher plant (*Cephalotus follicularis*), which is found in southwestern Australia.

Passive pitfalls

Unlike other carnivorous members of the plant kingdom, pitchers are passive plants. They do not actively catch their victims with dramatic, fast-acting traps. Instead, they lure their insect prey onto the top of the steep walls of their pitchers with strong odors and secretions of nectar. Some species, such as the California pitcher plant, have bright, translucent patches on the inside of the pitcher walls, which may disorientate the prey. Once at the top of the pitcher the unfortunate insect loses its footing and plunges down to the bottom of the pitcher, unable to grip the slippery sides. A mass of long,

NATURAL HABITAT

☐ California pitcher plant

downward-pointing hairs stop the insect from climbing out. Eventually, the poor creature drowns in a deep pool of liquid digestive acids that help the plant absorb the insect's body.

Pitcher lodgers

Although adult insects do not have a chance of surviving the digestive acids and enzymes in the fluid at the bottom of a pitcher plant's deadly trap, it seems that some insect larvae, such as those of mosquitoes, can live there. Here they can exist in a protected environment, and they are well fed on the bacteria and microscopic animals called protozoans found in the liquid. Similarly, tree frogs often use pitchers as brooding containers for their eggs, which are undamaged by the acidic broth.

Plants in danger

Like other carnivorous plants, such as the Venus flytrap and certain species of bladderworts, many pitcher plants are in danger from overcollection and loss of habitat. The California pitcher plant is now found only in a few wetland regions of California and Oregon. It has been officially classified as a threatened species by the U.S. Fish and Wildlife Service.

Tropical cousins

By far the most bizarre and fascinating pitcher plants are the *Nepenthes* pitchers, which are mainly found in the hot, humid tropical rainforests. Many of these are climbing plants, with thick, woody stems up to 1 in (2.5 cm) in diameter. They climb through the dense forests by means of long, thin, modified leaves called tendrils. The pitchers, which are held upright from the ends of drooping tendrils, become vastly inflated and hollow, looming through the trees like huge, garishly colored saxophones.

◀ *A pitcher plant (Nepenthes sp.) is split open to reveal the partially digested remains of insects.*

KEY FACTS

● **Name**
California pitcher plant or Cobra lily (*Darlingtonia californica*)

● **Range**
Wetland regions of northern California and southern Oregon

● **Habitat**
Wetlands such as marshes, swamps, and along riversides

● **Appearance**
Tall, narrow pitchers formed from long, greenish-yellow leaves, with a snake-like forked "tongue" emerging from the pitcher's opening and a brightly colored, hooded head covered with translucent (almost clear) "windows;" may grow to 3 ft (0.9 m) high

● **Life cycle**
Perennial

● **Uses**
Ornamental and novelty interest

● **Status**
Threatened

See also **Bladderwort, Venus flytrap, Wetland**

Index

Page numbers in **boldface** type show full articles